I'm no Shakespeare

Walking the South West Coast Path

Cheryl Dummer

The unlikely, but perfectly true story of how a nosey menopausal linguist threw away her pills, pulled on a backpack, and accidentally wrote a best seller.

This book is dedicated to my sisters, and to my feet.

Disclaimer

Some names and identifying details have been changed to protect the privacy of individuals.

Copyright © 2023

All rights reserved. This book or any portion thereof may not be reproduced or used in any manner whatsoever without the express written permission of the publisher except for the use of brief quotations in a book review.

Introduction

I was an odd child who wrote poetry and wanted to be Tarzan.

I would swim underwater for as long as possible on one breath, a plastic knife tucked into my knickers.

I climbed trees with my imaginary cheetah, practicing my Tarzan call, and nailing scraps of wood to branches to make one sided, roofless huts.

Goodness knows how many more chimps I have kissed since then, but now, as I walked, it was those days of innocence that I recalled.

I was born in a small South Devon village in November 1966, on my mother's twentieth birthday.

My parents had moved to Devon from Surrey for my father's work.

My Daddy.

Always 'Daddy'.

He died of leukemia just before my third birthday and never lived to be just 'Dad'.

I do not remember him, but what memories, Daddy, did you take with you?

Of your funny little girl.

I was twenty when I met and married Paul, in Plymouth where we both had bedsits.

Our daughter was born six months later, followed two years later by our son.

Paul maintained graveyards, and I was a chambermaid, half way through a gap year that had gone progressively wrong since I had arrived in New York the day after my final A level exam.

I had been a plain and studious Grammar school girl, with permanently inky fingers and most of the time with my head in a French textbook.

I was not one of the cool girls who ignored the school uniform rules, and who hung around the long-haired boys with their motorbikes.

Paul had been one of those boys, but I had neither known him nor noticed him.

Those girls would never have believed that, within five years, Paul would be marrying Cheryl, and that Paul's mum would be blow drying his hair before he walked down the aisle.

We divorced three years later, and Paul was just forty four when he died from a medical emergency related to his alcoholism.

I had always chased excitement.

I signed up for a course to become a pool lifeguard when I was thirty two, with no intention of actually working as one.

I passed with flying colours, despite my backwards breaststroke kick being weaker than that of the other candidates.

So I volunteered, at the ambulance training college in Chippenham, during an evening of water rescue training, to demonstrate a deep water rescue.

John, who I had only just met, played the role of the casualty

Jumping into the water beside my face down patient, I proceeded to execute a text book first half of the rescue.

Which consisted of turning him, by holding his chin and the back of his head whilst clamping my forearms to his back and chest.

And hugging him tightly to my breasts.

The next step was where my pathetic backwards breaststroke kick started to let me down.

Thinking on my feet, metaphorically because both mine and John's feet were dangling in the deep end at this point, I whispered in John's ear.

"You had better kick your legs, or I will pull your trunks down"

John played his role perfectly.

I retained my professional reputation and he, for a while longer at least, retained his personal modesty.

John and I married in 2002, and in 2020 we emigrated to our second home, close to a ski resort in a small mountain village in Bulgaria

John has now retired after thirty four years as a Paramedic, and I had been dismissed, after twenty years as an Emergency Ambulance Technician.

I had joined the ambulance service in January 2000, in the days before degrees in Paramedic Science.

The only way into the service then was to be accepted into the non-emergency patient transport service.

Once accepted, with some experience behind you, and if you could pass further exams, assessments, and interviews, you would win the opportunity to be sent away for eight weeks to an intensive ambulance training college in Chippenham.

I was a thirty three year old mother of three and competition was stiff.

Most people failed the fitness test.

I was determined to succeed, and I trained by walking each day, carrying a heavy pack, to the top of the Dartmoor Tor nearest to my home.

As my colleagues and I became older, our patients became heavier.

Back and knee injuries were common.

But for a fifty year old woman I was doing quite well.

Until I chose ice skating as a midlife hobby.

A complicated shoulder fracture brought a sudden end to my career.

Leaving the ambulance service and a job that I loved had been a shock.

After a year of delayed NHS diagnosis and treatment, and stressful meetings with HR and managers, all options for alternative employment were exhausted.

The Trust's sickness policy was taken to its inevitable conclusion.

Retirement on the grounds of ill health.

Our children were adults and John was perfectly happy in our mountain village, concreting and doing stuff with gravel and weed membrane.

Which are quite possibly his favorite two words in the English language.

I wanted more.

More thrill and more danger.

More excitement, to fill the void of no longer working twelve hour ambulance shifts.

Languages had always excited me.

And the way that my character changes when speaking in a different language.

When I speak French I feel more seductively feminine.

When I speak German I feel, in an utterly convinced I am right sort of way, more masculine.

In Bulgarian I am argumentative, and far more nosey.

So I set my heart on learning Italian, convinced that speaking the Italian language would make me feel a magnificent blend of all of the above.

In 2021 I travelled from Bulgaria to Italy, to work for a long, hot summer on the Adriatic coast, as a private English teacher to two little sisters.

Then I travelled alone to Sicily.

In Sicily I rented a studio in the Centre of the madness of the city of Catania.

A city in the shadow of Mt. Etna, where the buildings are made from black lava, and the inhabitants drive as if being chased by a lava stream.

I flung wide open the old wooden double doors to a wrought iron balcony, and embraced the street noise of shouts, horns and sirens, and the aromas of street cooking.

I immersed myself in the language.

I laughed with people and at their reactions, as I grappled with trying to make my needs and thoughts understood.

I drank cappuccino and ate pistachio fondant filled croissants in piazzas, while reading children's story books in Italian.

In street restaurants I ate richly sauced pasta, delicious baked artichokes, meats, and salad, whilst drinking blood red wine and speaking in Italian with excitable waiters.

I learnt the vocabulary for flavors and colour by ordering gelato, and studied textbooks whilst listening to Puccini and Pavarotti.

Late at night, in bars, with Italian beer, fat green olives, and bowls of rich sauced pasta, I eavesdropped on street conversations.

Living in Italy and learning to speak the Italian language made me fat.

But it also filled every sense with beauty and romance, and gave me pure joy.

Life in a Bulgarian mountain village has a more gentle rhythm.

As soon as the snow starts to melt, preparation begins for the next long, hard winter.

Vegetable gardens are dug, the first young nettles of the year are gathered to add to soups and stews, and tiny mushrooms are harvested for omelettes and more soup.

Fallen wood is collected for kindling while it is still easy to spot, and firewood is ordered, chopped, stacked, and left to dry.

Tomatoes, red peppers and other vegetables are pickled to be preserved through the months of snow and ice, and fruit is sweetened and bottled using large pans of boiling water around outdoor fires.

Buckets of grapes, plums and apricots are taken to the village still to be turned into hard liquor.

I was urged by my Bulgarian neighbor, who never takes no for an answer, to create a vegetable garden of my own.

I threw myself at the task, losing blood, sweat and nails in the process, and my garden was truly beautiful.

I grew salad crops, beans, pumpkins, and herbs.

But there is too little excitement in gentle rhythm.

And I grew restless once again.

I had a old TEFL qualification, which ignited another thrilling idea to avoid becoming John's unpaid labourer.

I posted my profile on a Bulgarian teaching forum, and before long my diary was full with students wanting conversation practice.

I enjoyed lesson planning and, unlike my vegetable garden, the work was portable.

I travelled to the UK and, with my laptop, I continued to teach.

For a while at least, it seemed perfect.

Until mixing concrete began to seem glamorous.

And I accepted that, although I was good at it, I far preferred learning languages, and even lesson planning, to actual teaching.

While John had been busily laying a path, I had been beavering away on Duolingo, attempting to teach myself Turkish.

I had very quickly reached levels of sentence structure of such ridiculous complexity that they were begging to be practiced.

Turkey borders Bulgaria and can be reached easily in a little over three hours.

So I found a cheap EasyJet holiday to Dalaman in Turkey and flew there from Bulgaria, via Bristol.

The language was far trickier to learn than Italian, but for two weeks I wandered, like a Jehovah's Witness, around the orange blossomed streets of Dalyan.

With a missionary smile, and a phrase book tucked under my arm, I threw myself at the mercy of the locals.

For breakfast, under the gaze of two thousand year old rock carved tombs of Thracian kings, I practiced ordering sweet, sludgy coffee and sticky baklava.

I read signs in street markets, and bought individual apples and other fruits to invite simple conversation.

I walked amongst the ruins of an ancient Roman city, bathed in healing mud pools from the time of the Ottoman Empire, and jumped off boats to swim with turtles in thermal lakes.

And in steamy hammams, wincing whilst being sandpapered and sighing with the pleasure of being covered in hot foam, I pried vocabulary from muscled men in loincloths.

At one of the airports I passed through on my way back to Bulgaria I treated myself to an orange blossom eau de parfum.

Trying to hold on a bit longer to the intoxicating scent of Turkey.

During the winter I left John again.

While he was busy gathering bruises whilst learning to snowboard, I travelled to Burgas on the Black Sea coast.

Hoping to gain a qualification in a subject that interested me, and crucially to perfect my Bulgarian, I enrolled on a five week intensive one to one course to become a qualified masseuse.

I had already reached a passable level in Bulgarian before I began to spread baby oil, for the first of many times, over my teacher's very attractive body.

However, it was not his body that interested me, not entirely, but rather his advanced grammar.

For five weeks, in Bulgarian, I learnt anatomic terms and the theory of massage, and unlocked the secrets of Bulgarian prepositions.

And, like a Mirror Group investigative journalist, I scooped the entire life story of not only my teacher but of all his family and friends.

As soon as I returned to the mountains I bought my own massage table, and set to practicing my newly qualified skills on my husband's legs.

If it were not for his arthritic knees, casualties of his own thirty four years in the ambulance service, John would certainly have walked with me.

And I would have enjoyed his company.

Occasionally.

If he had his own tent.

And if he pitched far enough away to avoid me stabbing him with a tent peg.

John waved cheerily as I entered the terminal building at Sofia airport.

He was confident that, like a big dinner, my need for excitement and my menopausal rage could both, once again, be walked off.

Contents

DAY 1 1
Blister Free

DAY 2 4
Rescue

DAY 3 7
Convalescence

DAY 4 10
Carb Loading

DAY 5 14
Qigong

DAY 6 16
Let it breathe

DAY 7 20
Aussie Muse

DAY 8 27
The Black Slug

DAY 9 32
Goddess

DAY 10..40
Tarka Trail

DAY 11..45
Barbie

DAY 12..49
Clotted Cream

DAY 13..53
Wife Swap

DAY 14..62
Therapeutic Gait

DAY 15..70
Angels

DAY 16..83
Civilization

DAY 17..90
Sauna

DAY 18..92
Sloe Gin

DAY 19..96
Wild Camp

DAY 20..99
Cryptosporidium

DAY 21..102
Linda

DAY 22..107
Why?

DAY 23..112
Luxury

DAY 24 .... **116**
    Storm Antoni

DAY 25 .... **120**
    Waterproof Socks

DAY 26 .... **125**
    Nafa

DAY 27 .... **131**
    Adder

DAY 28 .... **136**
    Bottom Shaft

DAY 29 .... **139**
    Penelope

DAY 30 .... **145**
    Zennor

DAY 31 .... **147**
    Pendeen

DAY 32 .... **150**
    Copper Kettle

DAY 33 .... **155**
    Lands' End

DAY 34 .... **158**
    Markus

DAY 35 .... **162**
    Slate Heart

DAY 36 .... **166**
    Lizard

DAY 37 .... **170**
    Dingo Den

DAY 38 .... **173**
    Fog Horn

DAY 39 .... **176**
    Half way

DAY 40 .... **180**
    Our Country's Moat

DAY 41 .... **183**
    Cappuccino

DAY 42 .... **186**
    Anthony
    The Pause Between Walking *189*

DAY 43 .... **193**
    Hypoglycemia

DAY 44 .... **197**
    Hannibal

DAY 45 .... **199**
    Doberman Church

DAY 46 .... **203**
    Ship Tracker Jo

DAY 47 .... **206**
    Plymouth

DAY 48 .... **210**
    Night Crossing

DAY 49 .... **212**
    Roscoff

DAY 50 .... **215**
    Ferryman

DAY 51 220
Trench

DAY 52 224
Hold on Tight

DAY 53 226
Rescue?

DAY 54 228
Gertrude

DAY 55 232
Spear Gun

DAY 56 235
Save Our Pub

DAY 57 237
Stealing from a Charity

DAY 58 242
Cabaret

DAY 59 245
Freedom

DAY 60 247
Roseships

DAY 61 250
Quality Holidays

DAY 62 253
Hero Dog

DAY 63 256
Poacher

DAY 64 260
Jungle

DAY 65 262
    Hermione

DAY 66 266
    Chesil Beach

DAY 67 270
    Bubble Bath

DAY 68 272
    Portland

DAY 69 275
    Rest Day

DAY 70 277
    Smugglers

DAY 71 281
    A Canoe of my Own

DAY 72 284
    Headspace

DAY 73 286
    Trust the Path

DAY 1

Blister Free

Less than twenty four hours later I stood beside the monument to mark the start of the six hundred and thirty mile long South West Coast Path.

The UK's longest hiking trail.

Three decades ago, with two weeks of precious freedom, and a two year old boy, I had left Plymouth to walk as far west into Cornwall as possible, along the same path.

Dogger had been our disobedient, imaginary dog.

Dogger would squeeze, muddy pawed, into our tent, steal ice cream, and shake seawater over sunbathers.

My son, his pockets filled with the treasure of shells, sea glass, tiny pebbles, and seabird feathers, would race Dogger to be the first to climb over stiles.

Carrying a small boy on the coast path was perhaps doomed to failure.

I'M NO SHAKESPEARE

As a single woman I could have seen off the unwanted attentions of an older male walker.

But with responsibility for the safety of a small child, I abandoned our tent and fled.

My son is a man now and has a funny little girl of his own.

Time may not have stood still, and its sands, like my hair, may have become a little finer.

But I was back, excited to try again.

And the sound of the sea had not changed.

My mind was a gloriously blank page, and my goals were simple.

To avoid blisters.

To avoid getting lost.

To not give up.

And, wherever possible, to avoid men.

I had barely left Minehead when, like a spider in its newly spun web, the first man I met attempted to capture me with his sticky threads of unsolicited advice.

I was ordered to take buses around urban areas.

And, apparently, I was using my poles completely incorrectly.

Like a stubborn three year old, or a recalcitrant wife, I completely ignored him.

In Porlock, as I was reposing in the grass beside my tent, I examined my bare feet.

I'M NO SHAKESPEARE

I was delighted to be blister free, and to have survived a nasty trip over my own poles.

I watched as a dog, on a last evening walk around the campsite, followed a scent, a zigzagged trail, nose down, towards my feet.

Then I watched as it simultaneously sniffed my socks, and urinated against my leg.

For good luck, I trusted.

DAY 2

Rescue

I gently removed a snail from my groundsheet, and boiled water.

A morning coffee had become a habit.

A habit acquired not only from Italy, but from Bulgaria.

In Bulgaria, where every street corner has a coffee machine, and where the national breakfast is an espresso and a cigarette

On the pebbled ridge of Porlock beach, a second dog, evidently confused over whether I was human or lamppost, sniffed, and lifted a leg.

Its owner apologized.

I continued through woodland, with the constant reassuring whoosh and pause of the sea always on my right.

If only the sound of my husband snoring were as soporific as the sound of the sea, we might not be sleeping in separate bedrooms.

Like having full faith in a deity, or in a bungee rope, I placed all my trust in my own forward motion, however slow, and in the path.

When Lynmouth finally came into view I felt exhilarated.

I'M NO SHAKESPEARE

However, the more I walked downhill towards the small town, the further it seemed to recede, until it took on the shimmer of a desert mirage, and I began to fantasies of an oasis with belly dancing camels and robed men in turbans, eating dates.

Finally, after my telephone call to the campsite that I had planned to stop at went unanswered, I realized that there was to be no desert welcome for weary travelers.

Even the public toilets were out of paper.

So I continued, and climbed steeply out of the town, then followed the coast path that ran perilously close to the cliff edge, towards the majestic Valley of the Rocks.

A storm forecast had been issued for strong winds and rain by dawn, and I began to feel the urgency to find a safe camp.

I continued past the last house in Woody Bay, soon to be far from human habitation, and guiltily picked raspberries from the edge of its private garden.

"Hey!"

A stern shout from behind stopped me abruptly.

A man, about my age, was walking towards me.

"It's a bit late for you hikers to still be out!"

I was in no physical condition to deal with any threat in any other way than a dog, who might lie submissively flat on its back, and wag its tail.

So, wiping raspberry juice hurriedly from my mouth, I explained my situation.

I'M NO SHAKESPEARE

With kind amusement, and without hesitation, he offered to drive me to a campsite, and invited me into his garden to meet his wife, bizarrely apologizing that she was barefooted.

A perfectly serene, barefooted lady, wrapped in a beautiful woolen poncho, greeted me kindly, and offered me a drink.

On the terrace table stood a bottle of wine, and a glass bowl of nuts.

The view across treetops towards the sea was all the more stunning from the comfort of their garden furniture at sunset.

Their pets, however, were showing an alarming interest in my trousers.

Not wanting to appear rude by kicking the two dogs away, and with my fingers firmly crossed that this information would not invalidate the offer of a lift in their brand new Mercedes, I explained my previous unfortunate canine encounters.

Fortunately it did not, and I soon found myself at a farm campsite, picking my way gingerly across a charcoal cratered battlefield, where barbecues and fires were freely permitted.

I pitched beside a low hedge, as near to the shower block as possible, and had no sooner pulled all my kit inside my tent than the first of three days of heavy rain showers began.

After a hot shower, in an open cubicle where birds nested, and defecated, from the rafters above my head, my muscles finally began to relax.

According to my telephone I had been walking for thirty two km, and I was so very grateful to such kind strangers for having spotted and interrogated me, and for having brought me to safety.

DAY 3

Convalescence

The campsite became my convalescent home.

A convalescent home for a bad weather stranded walker, battling with day three delayed onset muscle soreness.

Waking with a headache that made me wonder whether gin may have been added to last night's tea, I opened one eye to see that it was only 0600.

I needed to use the toilet.

I had an all-purpose plastic beaker which had worked well on my first night, before every muscle in my body had seized.

Now, manoeuvring both legs from my warm sleeping bag was slow and painful.

I yelped as the cold slugs that had attached themselves unseen to the rim of my beaker, made contact with my warm skin.

They too no doubt retracted in horror.

I'M NO SHAKESPEARE

I put on my glasses to inspect more closely, and saw that an entire squadron of the fattest and meanest looking slugs had taken up residence on my ground sheet.

Their forward advance had only been thwarted by my sleeping pod basin and bug net, which thanks to all Gods in all Heavens I had remembered to fully zip before sleeping.

Thirst for water and a need for caffeine, and a realization that one of my tent pegs had broken free, lured me out of my bag for the second time.

With a full set of waterproofs pulled on slowly over my merino wool pyjamas and down fleece, and with Crocs on my bare feet, I crawled out of my tent, repositioned the peg, and hobbled, Quasimodo style, towards the onsite cafe.

From the comfort of a dog scratched leather sofa I cradled a coffee, delighted to have found an electric socket, and I watched as the storm strengthened.

As my telephone sprang back to life I started to read news of European heat waves, funny family speculation over how and where I was, and a local weather forecast predicting even stronger wind for the next day.

The weather was out of my hands, and there were worse places to be, so I ordered a Big Barn Breakfast, and spent my morning in the cafe, reading, writing, and growing steadily stiffer.

I met a fellow armchair linguist, about my age, similarly windswept, and sheltering while her husband played whack a mole with their tent pegs in the camping field.

We drank coffee beside the wood burner, and chatted like sisters, then drank tea and ate cake.

I'M NO SHAKESPEARE

I bought an eye-wateringly expensive packet of cheap tent pegs from the shop, to attempt to put up my own double defence against the worsening storm.

And, having drank far too much tea, I hobbled painfully back and forth to the shower block.

After dinner, I again could barely stand, but a hot shower restored just enough muscle movement to once more collapse into bed, slug protection fully in place.

To the sound of sheep bleating from a nearby field, and rain hitting my tent, I fell asleep for the third night in my teepee-like home, and prayed for it to survive without losing any more of its pegs, without which the center pole would not hold.

DAY 4

Carb Loading

The slugs must have decided to stay away from the frightful screaming woman, and likely slugged off instead to investigate the less hysterical Germans, who had arrived the previous evening to pitch their two small tents in the far corner of the field.

It was July, so despite the strong Atlantic storms that were slowing my progress, the rain was at least warm.

Why then did the ground still feel as hard as an icy pavement, with its cold permeating my right hip and causing a deep ache that once started could not be eased without heat and movement.

The extra flesh that now padded out my fifty six year old hips should logically have acted as an insulator, but sadly did not.

My modern inflatable mattress had been recommended to me as far superior to the indestructible sponge mat that I had used thirty years ago, when my joints were younger.

The inflatable mattress was however only comfortable and warm when it lay directly under my body, and not when it was migrating around inside my bivvy bag, as if deliberately trying to suffocate me.

It was hard to believe that I was such a wriggly sleeper, when my sleeping bag held me like an Egyptian mummy, with barely any room to wriggle a big toe, let alone a hip.

And yet, another morning of waking with my nose pressed against its waffled surface while, like a blind underground mole, I felt every vibration of my straining tent pegs.

According to my sister, the remedy for my continuing stiffness was yoga,

But breakfast first, and my instant porridge sachets were eclipsed by a huge bowl of organic rolled oats with cinnamon, honey, and clotted cream.

With the wind speed forecast to reach fifty five kph, with accompanying torrential rain, continuing to walk was totally out of the question.

I either stayed and waited for the weather to improve, or I quit.

And I was certainly not about to quit.

At least not yet, not with such wonderful breakfasts.

If I could just find some Velcro for my inflatable tormentor, all would be perfect.

So, back to stealth stretching from a two seater sofa squashed beside a grumpy lurcher.

A lurcher who was used to having the whole sofa to himself, and who was more than a little displeased to be sharing his bed with a mere camper.

I'M NO SHAKESPEARE

A mere camper who, to a sensitive canine nose, probably still smelled like a lamp post.

Ankle onto opposite knee, pushed down and held.

Arms high above shoulders, stretched back to touch the wall.

Good grief, what pain, what addictive, pain relieving pain.

The grunting coming from the strange stretching lady on the sofa effectively cleared the cafe of its remaining breakfast guests.

All retreated no doubt to the comfort of their all in one, slug proof, and standing room tents.

And to their cosy caravans and camper vans with furniture, heaters, and kettles.

My new friend and her husband had applied for a last minute pet sitting position, and had been successful, so they packed and set off to drive through the storm to a warm house in the Cotswolds.

The chef strolled over to the sofa and whispered conspiratorially, as he collected my porridge bowl, that he was preparing a thick goulash.

I stayed to await his goulash and read.

In the afternoon, having walked through wet grass, and bitterly regretting my decision to wear socks with my Crocs, I bumped into another man.

Don, my age, was standing straight and tall beside a refrigerator, in the camp kitchen.

He was trying not to smile, with one arm held straight out in front of him.

I'M NO SHAKESPEARE

Apologizing for the obscenities that I had been hurling at the holes in my Crocs, I listened politely and offered assistance, as Don explained about his mislaid passport, and how he was trying to take a new photograph that would be accepted by the passport office.

I was neither afraid of walking in cold weather, nor in wet weather, and my new down jacket and waterproof coat had already fully proven their insulating and waterproofing properties.

However, the storm lashing the South West was bringing extreme gusting winds and heavy rain that threatened to breach both warmth and dryness simultaneously.

Cold and wet combined would be a recipe for disaster.

So, taking into account my destabilizing backpack and my less than perfect pole planting, it really did seem wise to remain patient.

And to concentrate instead on the vital task of loading as many more carbs as possible.

DAY 5

Qigong

The previous evening I had removed my inflatable mattress from inside my bivvy bag and placed it directly onto the groundsheet.

The position to which I suspected it had been fighting me to escape, knowing more about camping than I did.

Despite the dampness and the falling temperature, I had finally slept peacefully and undisturbed by my aching hips.

Emerging from my tent on my third morning of enforced rest, I was greeted by the first small patch of blue sky since the storms had begun.

Don, who was an artist, lived in a caravan on the site, and was busy clearing its gutter.

We greeted each other, discovering that we were both planning to walk to a nearby beach.

Me in physical and mental preparation for the next day, and Don to take some photographs for an art class that he would be teaching that afternoon, from his studio in Lynmouth.

I'M NO SHAKESPEARE

We walked together past the ponies, and the orchards, and through the stunted oak forest.

Then we followed a network of ancient trails downhill, until we reached the cove.

Don was kind and intelligent company, and he offered to teach me Qigong.

So, at the turning of the tide, on the hard, wet sand, beyond the rocks, we practiced the slow and deliberate movements of a martial art.

We felt the summer warmth on our bodies, as the sun began to shine and to remind us that it was still July.

I returned alone, past the oaks and the apple trees, impatient now to pull on my backpack and to rejoin the path.

From the camp shop I booked a taxi for early the following morning, to return me to the exact spot from where I had been rescued.

I should probably have done some laundry, but it was too late now, and wouldn't the ultra violet rays, surely soon to break through, clean my clothes?

DAY 6

Let it breathe

My sister is my biggest supporter and has full faith in me, continually sending me motivating messages, and very often advising me - at my own risk - on technical matters.

I had posted a photograph of my backpack, artfully positioned on a bench, next to my poles with a backdrop of blue sea and headlands.

"Take off its rain cover!"

She text barked at me.

"Let it breathe!"

Well, sis, I have no option now but to tell a little story about letting things breathe.

A story until now only shared with my lovely step daughter who, as a nurse and a midwife, I knew could be trusted not to snort to my face.

Who I trusted to give me some much needed emergency medical advice.

"Let it breathe!" brought the trauma back to me that Savlon has been thankfully easing over the last few days.

I'M NO SHAKESPEARE

Another nugget of sisterly wisdom, imparted before my walk, was to wear panty liners instead of knickers, to save weight.

This advice seemed very counter intuitive to me as I have never not worn knickers in my life.

Well, apart from when Belinda and I went skinny dipping in the Black Sea.

Or when Helen and I swam in the snow at midnight in January in hot spring pools in Bulgaria.

And when I was eighteen on the Appalachian Trail and was pulled by a boy to swim naked together in a thunderstorm.

It was an emergency, so may not count, but there was also a time with Rachel in Croatia, when my big pants were used to bandage my blistered foot.

And perhaps on that naturist beach I went to when I was sixteen where I burnt my bottom so badly that I had been unable to sit for a week, and had to keep making excuses for not making it to the dinner table.

But really, apart from those very, very few times, my knickers have been firmly in place in places where knickers should, for decency, be worn.

But my sister knows her stuff, and so I had packed some panty liners and duly attached their super-sticky strip directly to my trousers.

Sis, are you totally, totally mad?

My panty liners have been migrating in a feral manner that makes the tricks of my inflatable mattress seem cuddly in comparison.

I'M NO SHAKESPEARE

And the softest, uppermost skin of my innermost thighs, although toning up beautifully with all these hill climbs, has never known such trauma.

Not even when I misjudged the button lift three times in a row as a beginner skier did I feel such raw pain.

"Letting it breathe" sis, is exactly what I have been doing.

Knickers WILL be going back on, but not until I have fully recovered.

According to the law of gravity, what goes up must surely, like knickers, come down.

On the South West Coast Path the opposite holds true.

But how could a day, fuelled on clotted cream porridge, not be fantastic.

Like kittens chasing reflections, the sun chased away the shadows cast playfully across the sea by the clouds.

I applied sun protection, an Ambre Solaire which on its own had a most pleasing scent, but when combined with Lynx Africa became weaponized.

When I chose the contents of my wash bag I did not choose wisely.

My decisions were entirely emotional.

'Lynx Africa' had a ring of the exotic traveler.

A wild cat, light on its paws, roaming the plains or jungles of the mighty continent.

In reality I now smelled like a teenage boy, but without the hormones to give me at least an air of deadly predator.

I'M NO SHAKESPEARE

After many steep climbs and long descents, including to the summit of Great Hangman, I arrived at Watermouth Valley Camping, where I pitched next to a blackberry bush.

Dark purple and plump from the rain, but still tart, not yet sweetened by the sun.

I ate a few, nevertheless, to add a healthy supplement to my forward motion fuelling, flapjack based diet.

I discarded the Lynx in the communal shower products bucket.

DAY 7

Aussie Muse

Firstly, an apology to my sister.

It has become apparent that the error was all mine.

Her clear instructions were to put 'inside of' and not, as I with almost deadly consequences must have misheard, 'instead of'.

A firm line has now been drawn under the whole incident, never more to be spoken of.

Except that I have been thinking.

People are prepared to pay more and more for ultralight equipment, with modern lightweight carbon fiber walking poles costing at least two hundred pounds.

But monks on pilgrimages used stout wooden canes, and soldiers and early explorers wore heavy woollen clothes.

Before starting to walk, I had taken more sisterly advice, and had bought an ultra-lightweight umbrella from a specialist outdoor store.

It had cost twenty nine pounds.

I'M NO SHAKESPEARE

In the hiking world, the lighter things are, the more people are prepared to pay for them.

I recently saw a much sturdier looking brolly, not so many grams heavier, in a corner shop, for sale for three pounds and fifty pence.

Are we being had?

Perhaps we only need to train harder, to become less sedentary, to be able to carry heavier loads.

As Hele bay appeared over the headland, and while I was still buzzing high on a breakfast of sugary machine latte and sticky iced almond flapjack from the Watermouth Valley camp shop, I met my Australian muse.

Tall, strong, tanned, larger than life, all sun bleached twinkles, and perfectly stubbled.

He was through-walking the path from Poole, so almost at the end of his journey, having previously completed it my way round.

We stopped to chat, muttering about the constant chasing of electrical power that seems to conversely drain our own batteries at the same time as charging those of our telephones.

It was not like this thirty years ago, when I just waved goodbye and was off, out of reach.

In the time before telephone boxes were filled with books and turned into community libraries, when a public telephone was the only means of outside contact.

Or even twenty years ago, before sat nav, when each ambulance still carried street maps and hand drawn maps of rural areas

I'M NO SHAKESPEARE

According to my muse, the no-nonsense Australian approach to entering cafes, is to brazenly go in and scan the joint for sockets.

If there are no sockets, then to leave immediately.

If there are sockets, then to sit and to plug in your devices, without asking.

If it is not possible to do a scan then to ask staff if you may charge your phone.

If they say no, or give a 'lame' excuse, like it being against their insurance, then to leave immediately.

But, and this is the important bit, only after looking them directly in the eye, and saying:

(An Australian accent is optional)

"Look mate, I am not playing on social media here.

It is for my safety out there.

And I will hold you personally responsible if I fall off a cliff and have to be Helivaced".

At my next stop, in a cafe in Ilfracombe, I admit to bravely doing the Aussie first step of walking in and scanning.

There were no sockets, so I moved swiftly on to the second step of asking the staff.

And this is where my Englishness totally failed me.

On being told:

"No, I am sorry we have no sockets"

My mind totally blanked.

All I could reply was:

I'M NO SHAKESPEARE

"Oh, thank you"

"That's ok"

"You are so lovely here that I will order a coffee anyway".

My plan had been to continue to Woolacombe, and my legs were strong, but whispers had begun, on the wind from Ilfracombe, of a Shangri-La of campsites to be found on a hill before Wool Lacombe.

The whispers began in the cafe in Ilfracombe where I had stopped for a coffee and to search for a charging point.

There, I met the child catcher again.

An ultra-runner, about my daughter's age, and her partner, who had been at my previous campsite, the convalescent home, two evenings ago.

"I hate children" she had blurted out then, over a cider.

"Oh, are you a teacher?" I had asked politely.

"God no. I just hate children" was her reply.

As a mother of four I cannot in all honesty say that I have never had a single brief moment of hating children.

But her blanket assertion and her accompanying shudder made me feel quite unnerved.

It is like saying I hate old people.

Rude, and unnecessarily sweeping.

I thought of her again that evening when I saw a sign at the campsite, no doubt written for drivers, but ambiguous.

"Beware Children".

I'M NO SHAKESPEARE

In the cafe in Ilfracombe, Robert, my mother's age, had been eating gooey chocolate cake delicately with a fork, and had immediately engaged me in conversation.

Robert had just completed his laundry.

He always hand washes everything twice.

He had been to the dentist, and was enjoying his usual activities in his local cafe, where he was a well-known local.

Robert enjoys walking, and quizzed me about where I had been and to where I was headed.

"There is nowhere to camp in Woolacombe" he warned me.

"You must go to North Morte Farm".

He continued with emphasis, possibly sensing that I had a history of not always hearing accurately,

"Morte, M, O, R, T, E, like French for dead".

Robert used to be an electrical engineer, and he insisted on accompanying me to the high street, to help me to search for a fast phone charger.

I had made the mistake of packing my lightest phone charger, which also happened to be far slower at charging than a cafe coffee could acceptably be cradled, without needing to buy additional gooey chocolate cake and delicately pick up a fork.

Robert was a charming companion, telling me about his life and his medical history, and how he does not have a television because if he did he would "just watch it".

He kindly walked with me, climbing the steep old coach road out of Ilfracombe and pointing out his parent's old home.

I'M NO SHAKESPEARE

He wanted to clearly direct me back to the path, and he shared nuggets of his childhood experiences.

"You carry on ahead a bit dear"

He instructed, as we were half way towards the coast path, passing a field gate.

"I just need to cock a leg".

We parted a while later with genuine care, and the whispers of Morte Farm intensified as I walked.

Two groups of Germans, overtaking me as most people, especially Germans, seem to do, spoke in reverence of the shop there and of the views.

"How close is the site to the path?" I asked.

"Oh it's so close, you can see it from the path".

"And the shop is SO good".

So, on a bench above Lee Bay, trying to catch my breath, as the view below me and out towards the cliffs behind me threatened to take it away, I called North Morte Farm.

A very much alive lady answered me welcomingly, and assured me that yes there would be a patch of grass for the night for me to call home.

I did wish she had thought to mention pitching around the perimeter hedges, but I was positive that all may yet end well.

The rain had held off all day, and I set up camp in windless sunshine in the centre of a camping field, overlooking the sea and Lundy Island, and from where I planned to watch the sunset.

I'M NO SHAKESPEARE

I had not noticed, until emerging from the shower block into squally rain, and a grey sea merging rapidly into grey sky just beyond the cliff edge, that all the other tents were pitched beside the hedges around the field perimeter.

I was alone, unsheltered, and perched on the flattest area of the sloping field, above rabbit holes.

I feared another rookie error.

DAY 8

The Black Slug

I had wanted to write about the shop last night, but straight after becoming momentarily overcome with the choice of superlatives with which to describe it, my telephone battery had died.

I had spent the next hour and a half, with my disappointingly not so fast new charger, babysitting my mobile phone, alone in the camp laundry room.

To fill the time it took to reach just over sixty percent I practiced some more Qigong.

My deep squats were getting easier to hold, and, dare I say it, becoming quite a feature.

My frequent trail comfort breaks, whilst carrying a twelve kilogram pack, were evidently paying off.

My tent fared admirably under its unforecasted evening battering, and the clouds sitting above the horizon cleared just in time to see the golden ball of a summer sun drop into the sea.

I'M NO SHAKESPEARE

I however, dreamt fitfully of falling into the network of bunny burrows onto which I had camped, and of a giant double headed black slug chasing me down blind alleys.

I woke several times, wet with sweat, before realising that the sweating was more likely due to the waterproofs that I had gone to bed wearing, in anticipation of a midnight tent catastrophe.

Lundy, Lundy. A soft and romantic name, reminiscent of Scottish Highland islands and lochs, mysterious, bathed in low northern light and fine mist.

Lundy island had come into view yesterday as South Wales started to slip away, and the island had captured my imagination as I walked.

I had picked up a Lundy tourist leaflet in the laundry room the previous evening, and had devoured every word.

A pirate lair of old.

Home to black rabbits.

But today, during my eighteen km walk from North Morte to Croyde, slogging across Woolacombe Bay at low tide, lost in my thoughts, and with Lundy never out of my sight, the realisation had hit me.

Lundy was my slug.

My double headed, nightmare slug.

All day, from all directions it had swivelled and watched me.

This is no conjoined headed double head, where you may at least have a chance to escape into its blind spot and run.

I'M NO SHAKESPEARE

Oh no - this evil creature has a head at both ends, and swivels in the Bristol Channel, guarding and keeping its pirate secrets safe.

The Black Slug.

I recalled the map of the island from last night's leaflet.

Look at it.

There is no doubt.

I was in a hurry now, to round Hartland point, to leave Lundy, and to get myself far away, and into the land of Pixies.

But the words that had gathered all day in my mind as I walked were like butterflies waiting to be freed, and my mother needed to be shown evidence that I had been doing my laundry.

Blister inducing salt crystals had begun to form between my toes, and I had been warned by more experienced walkers of the dangers of dirty socks.

So it was time to rest again, for more than just one day, and to enjoy my first sea swim.

For two nights I stopped in Croyde, in the delightfully named Cherry Tree Farm.

The two smaller campsites I had arrived at first, had both been full.

The third was a large corporate holiday park, aptly named Ruda, where the charge was a non-negotiable seventy pounds for two nights, no car, one person, non-electric.

"Our pitches are priced by pitch, with electric, for up to four people", the less prickly of the two receptionists snapped, whilst typing on her computer with total indifference.

I'M NO SHAKESPEARE

The other simply wrinkled her nose rather too obviously in my direction, cementing my resolve to find a more welcome stop, and to start laundering.

Walking towards Cherry Tree Farm I passed Hervé, who was standing at the bus stop and thumbing a lift.

We exchanged a few funny words.

Hervé was trying to pass himself off to me as Australian, but was far too European, attempting a double cheek kiss but stopping at one and a half.

I think I detected another nose wrinkle.

Before leaving him I had held out my own thumb.

I am no Daisy Duke, but the next surfer van to pass stopped to offer us both a lift.

Hervé and I high fived our goodbyes, and I hobbled on.

At the farm gate a handsome surfer from Porthcawl answered my query about whether Cherry Tree Farm had a reception.

"Oh yes" he said, in his very attractive Welsh accent

"You just have to go through the bar area".

So off I had staggered, through the entrance field, where he had been taking a very visually appealing shower at the back end of his sex wax stickered surf wagon.

I was really looking forward to having a sit down in the bar area, and a pint.

But there was no sign of any bar area in front of the reception.

Just grass.

I'M NO SHAKESPEARE

And a barrier.

DAY 9

Goddess

Before this morning's unfortunate coffee making incident, I lay still in my warm cocoon, my muscles heavy and half paralysed with sleep, and with dappled daylight caressing my closed eyelids.

I was listening to melodious deep throated coos from a fixed position close by.

Coos that were answered in echo by the same sound, softer, from further away.

There was an occasional duck-like quacking from the direction of the empty field behind my tent.

And a staccato, high pitched trill came from what seemed to be all directions at once.

The morning orchestra was completed by the raucous calls of seagulls, and the far off shushing rhythm of waves hitting the shore.

My dead slow walking pace affords me time to observe many birds, insects and plants.

I'M NO SHAKESPEARE

I used to feel ignorant that I only knew the names of a few, for example gorse, heather, bracken, then a 'bird', a 'butterfly', a 'flower', or 'an insect'.

Compared to many, I know I am very ill-informed.

And yet, the more I walk among them, the more I realise that these creatures and plants, who seemingly thrive and who go about their business with such song and joy, do not know my name, or exact ethnic heritage, or self-identity either.

I am simply a 'human', and that is all they need to know.

In fact, I am a rather stupid water boiling human because I have just done what I knew was bound to happen sooner or later, and burnt my plastic bowl.

The plastic bowl that should always first be removed from its space saving home tucked over the bottom of my stove pan.

After disposing of my burnt plastic bowl in the camp recycling bin, and grinning at the wild eyed woman smiling back at me from the washroom mirror, I continued with my laundry.

The beach, and my first sea swim, were waiting, but despite my childless, wind kissed freedom on the path, domestic tasks required attention.

Initially, my wash bag had contained only the bare essentials of a toothbrush and toothpaste, a comb, a small bottle of shampoo, the now discarded Lynx Africa, a fleece tea towel, and an all-purpose bar of Coal Tar soap.

My lucky soap, whose magical powers I attributed to not having been bitten by any biting insect, not even once, since the start of my walk.

I'M NO SHAKESPEARE

It was in the shop at North Morte Farm, a shop full of every known vegan delicacy, and pumpernickel bread, that I had been attracted by the lighter weight of a lavender and geranium, all in one, combined bar of shampoo and soap.

I recalled Nooshka, my Bulgarian village neighbour, who knows every medicinal property of nettles, cucumber, and curds and whey, and who keeps geraniums in pots to deter mosquitos.

So, still in awe of the shopkeeper's story, a story which I will soon retell, I purchased the sweet scented product.

My backpack was lightened by another gram or two, my hair was wilder, but softer, and as a laundry product, the suds that this bar produced were impressive.

I hung my laundered walking trousers to dry, to bathe in ultraviolet light, over the gate to the empty field.

And I swam, in the cold saltiness of the Atlantic.

My dry bag rested on my crocs at the water's edge.

My body stretched, and I was wearing a bikini for the first time in my life.

Well, OK, big pants and a sports bra.

I was freed from gravity's effects of carrying my heavy pack.

My toes spread in the grainy sand, and I sang to myself, making up words and trying to find rhymes.

Float... boat... coat... goat...

I stopped as I made the connection, and I started to laugh.

Crazy singing woman alone in the sea, far away from the orange and yellow flags between which the sign had said I MUST swim.

I'M NO SHAKESPEARE

What if, today, with my trousers on the gate, they decided to put goats in the empty field?

I strode out of the sea, strong and confident, a sea goddess, my thighs reflecting the strength gained through my walking, my soft belly proudly exposed, and my nipples almost as hard as the sand ripples created by the retreating tide.

I was ready to find a place to drink coffee and to write, to free my butterflies, and to observe the busy summer life of this small holiday town.

Thoughts of coffee soon evaporated on seeing a pub with a large teepee, and hearing relaxed surf music wafting across its adjacent beer garden.

This was to be my second creative space for the day.

A creativity to be encouraged by a pint of Tribute and a packet of salted peanuts.

Our youngest and naughtiest son, James, was not made for school, and he was educated at home from the age of ten.

He went alone, with his hand written CV, to a local donkey rescue sanctuary and asked to speak to the manager.

The manager asked him where his parents were, and James replied that his father was waiting in the car parking area outside.

It was explained to James' responsible adult that there was no official provision for volunteer work for a ten year old.

However, having been impressed by James' confidence and his obvious passion to gain experience working with animals, the manager had offered James the opportunity to attend for two mornings a week.

I'M NO SHAKESPEARE

Ostensibly, he would be under the umbrella of being a child with special needs, and therefore eligible for donkey 'therapy'.

In reality, the boy was handed a man's shovel and permitted to work alongside the mainly older women volunteers.

There James stayed for several years, learning about donkey care and behaviour, and progressing to supporting other young people who attended for riding therapy.

The shopkeeper in the shop at North Morte Farm, although my age, reminded me so much of my son.

At a similar age, growing up in Swindon, far from the sea, he had watched a documentary about a famous Hawaiian surfer known as the Duke.

A small boy, watching open-mouthed the grace of wave riding men.

And he dreamt.

At age seventeen the boy was almost a man.

He caught a bus from Swindon to Woolacombe, headed straight for the beach, and sought out the surfers.

With a passion and a desire to learn to surf, and a job found, with accommodation provided, in a local hotel, he quickly became proficient and addicted to the freedom of the sport.

Now he is a portrait artist who also hand produces beautiful bespoke wooden boards.

He still surfs daily, his warm character sharing some of the magic of the open sea and sky.

I'M NO SHAKESPEARE

There are some days that you never want to start, and some that you want to never end.

My day in Croyde was of the latter kind.

A veritable good witches' brew of sunshine and sea swimming, real ale and fish and chips.

Even on my rest day, my feet had been massaged kindly for almost nine km by the tiny insole bumps of my happy turquoise Crocs.

Brightly dressed parents pulled their filled to the brim beach trolleys.

Wandering amongst them I heard snatches of conversations, as teenage girls threw chips to the seagulls, whilst covertly trying to attract the attention of the lifeguards:

"Do you want a Vegan Magnum?"

"Mummy, what is Glamping?"

Resting on a dry stone wall, my legs dangled as I savoured the deliciousness of every mouthful of my fish and chips.

A little boy, perhaps four years old, walking along the sandy path from the beach and holding his mother's hand, suddenly spotted my Crocs.

"Mummy!" he exclaimed excitedly.

"Those Crocs are the same colour as mine!"

"Oh my goodness!" I said to him as he passed by.

"We have the same colour Crocs!"

"My Crocs are so happy to see yours!"

I'M NO SHAKESPEARE

He smiled and air wiggled a foot in my direction, as my own feet danced back.

Sun and schools are out for summer, and that 'first day of the holidays' feeling is infectious.

Laying in my bug proofed inner sanctum a little after ten pm I heard discussion from an adjacent pitch, where a family had newly arrived.

Two young children, perhaps eight or nine years old were still nowhere near ready for bed.

"Is it a tent or a Pyramid?"

"Touch it!"

"No, you touch it!"

"Ok, come on, shhhh!"

The braver of the two approached my tent slowly, whispered on by his sister.

His tip toe shadow was visible through my single skin tarp, looming towards my lair.

I waited, holding my breath, until the moment of dimpling touch.

Then, madly, impetuously, without thinking of the consequences, I roared.

The deep throated, spine tingling roar of a lioness protecting her cubs.

A blood curdling roar that echoed around the site, reaching down to the bay dunes and startling the lifeguards and the teenage girls.

I'M NO SHAKESPEARE

The children scarpered, screaming, and I stifled giggles.

I heard them dramatically re-enacting my roar to their parents.

Then, safely gathered inside their own tent and away from the Egyptian Lioness, the night fell silent.

The lioness slept deeply.

DAY 10

Tarka Trail

At 0800 she packed away her pyramid, and double clawed a winking warning to the two bed headed children, who were already nervously picking up their water pistols.

I wove between early holidaying joggers and dog walkers, in search of coffee and carbohydrates.

Nowhere was yet open and, thanks to a restaurant sign that was advertising 'Cream Teas to Curries, Moules to Martinis', my appetite dulled.

I walked on to stop at the first sea salt gnarled bench, overlooking Saunton Sands, and nibbled at a peanut flapjack.

I am no podiatrist, or proctologist either for that matter, but I seemed to have been cursed by the twin afflictions of Lazy Arch and Lazy Arse.

Attributed no doubt to nine km wearing Crocs, and quite possibly to the Tribute.

I headed off again, in the direction of the beach cafe at Saunton Sands, passing the imposing edifice of the Saunton Sands Hotel.

I'M NO SHAKESPEARE

I paused to walk slowly and to chat with a radiantly happy looking elderly couple walking hand in hand away from the hotel.

The wife told me that she had grown up in Westward Ho! Where, as a girl, she had gazed out of her bedroom window in awe at the lights of the huge hotel on the cliffs across the bay.

And now, for their diamond wedding anniversary, she had brought her husband there, to finally stay in the hotel of her childhood dreams.

I always read the engraved inscriptions on benches, and they often make me cry.

I was reminded of this one, which I had photographed, on a plaque on a high coast path bench just before reaching Croyde.

In 1976, in memory of his wife Marjorie, Henry Lewis Spink had written the following verse:

Rest here belovēd in your new life and behold
As oft you did with me when in the old
The majesty and power of which you now are part
And i will come and ease my aching heart

The importance of starting the day adequately hydrated cannot be overemphasized.

Realizing that I had omitted to drink my usual five hundred ml bottle of water before leaving Lion camp, I immediately guessed the main reason for my morning idleness.

A good intake of water later, with my resolve further strengthened by coffee, and with a hot steak pasty tucked safely into the top of my pack, I set off from the busy kiosks of Saunton beach.

I'M NO SHAKESPEARE

I sauntered happily along the tracks through the sand burrows, and across the golf course towards the Taw estuary.

My feet once more followed the meditative rhythm and pace, metronomically set by my poles.

Butterflies appeared randomly, often in pairs, their joyful dance a true fairy godmother to me.

I talk to them, grateful for every colourful flutterby.

In a car park, at the entrance to the Taw, a perfectly positioned bench became both my restaurant seat and my table.

The finest Pasty dining experience.

The only way to reach the far side of this large tidal estuary is by foot.

An initial elevated path overlooks drunken, paint chipped wooden boats and houseboats that wait lopsidedly in the mud for the incoming pull of the tide.

Then, from Braunton, there is a long tarmac trail, The Tarka Trail, which is shared with cyclists and day walkers.

Walking on such a hard surface over such extended distance and time caused a sharp pain to develop along a muscle in my left shin.

Niggle turning to gnaw, I began to limp.

I chose a public Spotify song list entitled 'South West Coast Path' and tucked my mobile phone into my waist pouch.

Speaker upward, I walked and listened.

Tears silently appeared as I bore down on Barnstaple.

I'M NO SHAKESPEARE

Not from sadness, nor from pain, and certainly not from Barnstaple, but from the music and the beauty of the lyrics.

Despite my painful limp, I continued over the Taw Bridge, and commenced shuffling slowly along the opposite side of the estuary, back towards the sea.

I have only once before had reason to employ my threatening, Warrior Woman double pole plant.

A strong and fearless 'mess with me at your own risk' stance, that aims to scare off all but the very stupid.

Who I would then kill, viciously.

On being approached by a particularly menacing looking, gloved and hooded cyclist, as I was trying to put as much distance as possible between myself and Barnstaple, I practised my third, improved, version.

I passed Fremington Quay where fish and chips were being eaten from cars, and where the cool evening estuary breeze was beginning to strengthen.

After a final mile I arrived, emotionally and physically exhausted, at Tarka Trail Campsite.

With my pyramid secured, and far more sensibly positioned for protection from the oncoming weather, I staggered unsteadily towards the Bistro Brewery next door, missing the stability of my metal front legs.

Two ladies, appalled at the starved dog glance I threw towards their table, benevolently tossed me a slice of their pizza.

Gratefully, I lurched onwards towards the bar, where I ordered a pint of Exmoor Ale, and chased it down with ibuprofen.

I'M NO SHAKESPEARE

Warm and safe in my tent, my lavender and geraniumed body was clean and fully relaxed after the longest and hottest shower, and I finally closed my eyes.

DAY 11

Barbie

I had fallen asleep to the vibrations and to the sound of galloping hooves, and to the wild mane shaking whinnying of a Black Beauty, freed for the night in the field directly behind my tent.

Memories of a twelve year old girl, saving her pocket money a month at a time, to exchange for an hour of horse riding from a stables on the edge of Dartmoor.

I would cycle there and back, and often stop on my way home to rest my bicycle against a field gate, climb its rungs, and lay, hidden, chewing on long grass, watching the clouds.

The rain started, and I realised that pitching under trees had perhaps not been such a clever decision.

Even in the brief pauses between the rain showers, the summer leaves continued to drip, drip water onto my tent.

I decided to remain at Tarka Trail Camping for a second night, to allow an extra day for my shin to rest and to wait for the wet greyness to pass.

I'M NO SHAKESPEARE

And because I did not need much temptation to spend a second evening enjoying the smooth taste of Exmoor Ale.

The tide and sailing times of the Instow to Appledore ferry were also more perfectly aligned for the following morning.

So I dressed carefully, crouching low in the centre of my tent to pull on my waterproof coat and trousers, trying not to let any part of me touch any part of the wet sloping sides of my tent.

One thing I have learnt in life is that adventures do not happen to those who stay at home all day.

I would have to leave my shelter, and to face the rain.

At the bus stop, waiting beside me to catch the bus to Barnstaple, an elderly man was keen to chat.

Eric was widowed, and pulling a tartan trollied shopping bag.

He had been brought up in London, but recounted that both sets of his grandparents were "from the land", and it was from them that he proudly attributed his lifetime of contentment living here.

He told me that he had been living in his bungalow for fifty seven years, and that he loved the quiet pace of life.

And that he missed his wife.

In Barnstaple I waited in the rain for the cinema doors to open, stepping around the pavement puddles with the fathers and their children who were there for the Saturday cinema club.

The doors were eventually opened by bright smiling staff, who were dressed head to toe in Barbie pink.

I'M NO SHAKESPEARE

It was not a moment too soon for Rufus' father, whose son, becoming dangerously bored of waiting, had started to play an energetic public punch ball with his father's belly.

I secured the last remaining ticket for the afternoon's first showing of Barbie, and tucked it inside my dryest pocket, like a prized Chocolate factory Golden Ticket.

With three hours to kill until the pinkness began, I walked through the town, searching for shelter from the rain.

I passed a fresh fruit and vegetable shop, and filled my pockets with a peach, an apple, and more emergency flapjack.

A Wetherspoons caught my eye, and I gratefully entered its alternative, warm space universe for breakfast beer drinkers.

Forgoing the beer, and deciding guiltily to leave the fresh fruit in my pockets to ripen a while longer, I instead ordered a traditional breakfast with a refillable coffee, and I wrote.

Barbie, although I must warn women of my age to take a little less pre-screen advantage of Wetherspoons' refillable coffee, was a hilarious pink riot of a film.

Seeing so many groups of young teenagers brought back memories of having been twice to the cinema to see the musical film Grease when it was released in 1978.

My best friend, Sarah, and I had both watched wide eyed, and had learned by heart the lyrics to every song from the movie's soundtrack.

We had not understood the adult themes of the film, but had shared an experience that we would never forget.

I'M NO SHAKESPEARE

Back at the campsite it continued to rain, and my limp-sided tent was even more damp and uninviting.

I loitered around the shower block, like a teenager around the bike sheds, out for a sneaky snog or a cigarette.

There I struck up a conversation with Elton, who was my age and similarly loitering.

Elton was a retired policeman from Northern Ireland, a cyclist and boat skipper, who shared with his bicycle an even smaller tent than mine.

We entered the Bistro Brewery on the dot of its 1900 opening time, and set matches, not to secret cigarettes, but to a wood burner.

Our clothes dried next to the bone-entering warmth of the fire, and we spent the evening together, sharing pizza and beer, and stories.

DAY 12

Clotted Cream

The following morning, with the halcyon summer Goddess day in Croyde now far behind me, I Examined my reflection in the shower block mirror.

A collapsing centre pole in the early hours had left my hair in an even wilder state than usual, more Old Grey Mare than Black Beauty.

I set to taming it, and after cleaning with hand soap and repositioning my glasses, I spotted a small patch of blue sky over the Atlantic.

My plan was to complete the last section of the Tarka Trail, before catching a mid morning ferry from Instow across to Appledore.

So, with a fresh plaster on the beginnings of a blister, and the wind fully in my own sails, I shouted a final goodbye to the beautiful Irishman.

I'M NO SHAKESPEARE

Breakfasting on blackberries from beside the estuary, I revelled in never knowing what juicy burst of flavour may be squeezed out of each berry that I popped into my mouth.

Tart, wincing, underripe plum, or my favourite; a rich, smooth, full bodied Merlot.

I silently clinked my imaginary glass to the Weatherspoon's' breakfast beer drinkers.

Dagmar was my age, a software developer from a small village near Dresden.

Closing in on each other from opposite directions, we both smiled widely.

Coast path through-hikers are as instantly recognizable to each other as Eddie Stobart lorries, and we carry similar sized loads.

Dagmar was also walking alone, now on her forty fourth day, and we stopped to chat like long lost friends, comparing and giving tips on campsites, blisters, and husbands.

Disembarking from the ferry at Appledore, I waited on a bench on the quay, and ate the second of the two cinnamon swirls that I had bought on the Instow side of the ferry.

With the sweet, sticky cinnamon licked clean from my fingers, I wrote, and enjoyed the peace of the small town, a place of lightness and colour that lived up to the beauty of its name.

Colin the crab had a very tough life.

Of his four really quite simple requirements which are posted on the Appledore quay railings, I observed two being broken.

I'M NO SHAKESPEARE

1. I am not a social crab, so I prefer a bucket which is not overcrowded.
2. When your crabbing is done, I am not really a thrill seeker - I prefer a sedate entry back into the river from your bucket, at the water's edge please.

The boy changed his crabbing position frequently, seeking maximum exposure, and he boasted loudly, to other young crabbers, of the thirty three Colins, all fighting for space in his bucket.

I wandered for a while among the other children, peered into their buckets, and lent my nail scissors to a small boy who was struggling to open his pack of not for human consumption crab bait bacon.

He showed me his vial of super crab potion, and let me in on the secret that this potion, once added to his bacon, would be irresistible to all Colins, and would ensure that he would catch at least a 'zillion trillion' more Colins than anyone else.

We both ducked as thirty three Colins flew past us, ignominiously lobbed sideways back to the river from the highest point of the quay.

My new friend, Qigong Don, had been following my journey and encouraging me.

He was in the process of moving to Appledore to set up a studio, and had offered to meet me on the quay, and to treat me to coffee in a cake shop tucked along one of the town's narrow streets of brightly painted fisherman's cottages.

We laughed and shared more stories before Don walked with me to the end of the town, from where I set off alone to circumnavigate the Northam Burrows towards Westward Ho!

I'M NO SHAKESPEARE

An ice cream van, or to be more exact the words 'Clotted Cream' written on the side of an ice cream van, drew me to it like a snake charmer to a cobra.

Before I knew it the words "Please can I have the biggest cone you do, with two flakes and the hugest humanly possible dollop of clotted cream" had been hypnotically drawn from my mouth.

Westward Ho! a mini Blackpool, was no place to linger over coffee, so I grabbed a pasty and kept on walking.

The crumbling cliffs after Westward Ho! rolled more gently than the steep inclines and descents of Exmoor.

Over coffee with Don, I had promised to send some lyrics for him to put to music, so I sang to myself as I walked in the rain towards the evening's campsite at Westacott Farm.

DAY 13

Wife Swap

If you in any way value your sleep, then despite the near overwhelming temptation, it is never ever a good idea to attempt to ignore even the lamest of weak bleats from your bladder.

Nor is it ever sensible to in any way attempt to postpone the inevitable hellish ritual.

The ritual that begins with a wriggling self-rebirth from the womb-like warmth of your sarcophagus.

Progressing inexorably to an increasing double-handed panic to locate the zip to your bug-proofed inner sanctum.

(There are in fact two zips, but they hibernate during hours of darkness).

And finally, before having to do it all again in reverse, to execute a blind belly-crawl into the terror and chill of a post-apocalyptic, dark side of the moon, slug infested minefield.

On a dew filled morning, with lyrics completed to rival McCartney's, and dispatched to Don for him to turn into our respective fortunes, my Pyramid was again packed away.

I'M NO SHAKESPEARE

I damply set off in the direction of Clovelly, and of coffee, hosting the irritating torment of an evil Mull of Kintyre ear worm.

I was wearing full waterproofs, with a waterproof cover stretched tightly over my backpack, as I walked back down the lanes and through a gate to join a footpath back to the coast path.

While I was idly wondering whether there might exist such a thing as ultralight windscreen wipers for spectacles, I spotted a gorgeously logoed white van in a quiet layby.

'Salty Dogs Dog Walking and Sitting'.

How clever I thought, for van-lifers to disguise their homes in such a way.

Shortly afterwards, an even more gorgeous young woman, with two wet and happy dogs, stopped and stood aside to let my wide load pass.

She, I, and the dogs, greeted each other wetly and waggily.

Kim had started her business just before COVID, and, with the surge in dog ownership, it had flourished.

Her client list was full, and I understood her when she said that the best thing about her job was being outside all and every day.

Kim was also interested in my reasons for being out so early in such weather.

When I replied that I was heading for Clovelly, she drew a breath.

"It is ten long miles, and very up and down," she said.

My need for coffee and fuel would not last ten minutes, let alone ten miles.

I'M NO SHAKESPEARE

So, as the rain slowed and stopped, as the weather forecast had promised it would, I set up my stove on a bench that bore a thought provoking inscription written by Mark French:

"Sit long, talk much, laugh often".

I breakfasted on the coconut and 'vegan friendly' flapjack that I had bought two days ago in Barnstaple.

I was pleased to see it was vegan friendly, as it must be hard to be both vegan and to have no friends.

My trail flapjacks: almond, coconut, and my favourite peanut butter, have all been dear friends to me as I have walked, and I felt overcome with the need to write a song for them too.

Ode to my Flapjack (to the tune of "Galveston")

Flappy Jacks, O Happy Chaps,

> Do you hear my tummy rumbling?

> Do you see my fingers fumbling

> In my Fanny Pack

While sitting on the bench and drinking my coffee, from my dual purpose beaker, I received a WhatsApp message from my sister.

My sister suggested I need a marketing executive type literary agent and was putting herself forward, in a very pushy way, for the job, wanting to firm up a book title and also my next long distance hike.

My reply:

"Oh ffs it's a blog sis, not a book, and my writer's block is only just about being kept at bay by the rich story sources, and my dillydallying.

I'M NO SHAKESPEARE

If you want a title then it's 'The Whoosh Between Heartbeats', and you can Fuck Off with any other long distance hikes"

Please excuse my foul language.

I was sleep deprived.

My sister used to lecture in Public Services, and a myriad of other remedial subjects, to difficult to teach teenagers.

She was not fazed, and knew how to respond to such crassness.

"Will accept the Fuck Off. Literary agents / managers understand the extreme situations and hardship. How it affects our clients.

But get a grip. Guzzle more coffee and porridgey stuff.....Sharpen your ears and pencil..... Now on you go..."

Impressive.

I wondered whether I may in fact have the need of such a mighty agent.

Someone to watch my back, to say it like it is, and to give me a metaphorical kick when my energy and resolve inevitably start to slip.

That morning I had broken camp quickly to get away from Weird Dutchman.

I had first met Weird Dutchman while chatting with Dagmar yesterday.

He had been passing us both, coming from my direction.

In my excitement to see another Stobart I had blurted out an ill thought out invitation:

"Oh, hi!!!! Do you want to be in our gang?"

I'M NO SHAKESPEARE

He and Dagmar had looked at me, and then at each other.

They had exchanged a few words, Germanic, sotto voce, and Weird Dutchman had scuttled off towards Instow.

I had caught up with him at the ferry to Appledore, where he avoided eye contact and kept up the weirdness, even on the boat where we sat facing each other.

I am no Piers Morgan, and I am certainly no stereotypical English woman, but I will always smile and say hello to get a good story.

I had seen him again at the previous night's campsite.

An unmistakable figure.

Tall and lanky legged, which was the only Dutch thing about him.

Dressed in a black t-shirt and black leggings, with a mop of white hair and beard, and wearing bottle glasses.

The spit of Gerry Adams, and with a suspiciously enormous backpack, juxtaposed against his tight black leggings.

Once again, my presence had been ignored.

[Note to my agent: You may want to edit this bit sis for political incorrectness. I blame my evening of black humour with the Irish policeman].

Fortified with coffee and coconut flapjack, I continued along the cliff path that overlooked the wild and uninhabited length of Peppercombe beach.

The whoosh was strong there, as each wave forcefully met the pebbled shore.

I'M NO SHAKESPEARE

At the point where a short flight of wooden path steps met the beach I stopped to rest my pack against a large piece of bleached driftwood, and stood tall on the pebbled ridge.

Facing the morning swivel of Lundy, as if in deep Pagan worship, I began timing my breath to the sound of the sea, arms stretched outwards and up to the sky, horse stance, slowly drawing the bow.

Feeling at once energised and relaxed, I turned to reposition my pack on my shoulders.

And there, where the second set of wooden steps rejoined the path from the beach, I saw them.

Familiar legs.

Trotting quickly away from Weird Englishwoman.

Since the very beginning of my walk it had been my left leg that had had the twin niggles of a blister, and the painful anterior tibialis that had been exacerbated by the hard surface walking of the Tarka Trail.

Both ailments had thankfully soon resolved.

Now it was my right leg's turn to suddenly develop an inflamed anterior tibialis.

Tibialis sounds like a Roman emperor, but if he is then I can assure you that he is not one of the good ones.

My walking had become slower, at times threatening to shift into reverse.

I was grateful for the left leg's soldiering on, and taking the strain for his injured compatriot.

I'M NO SHAKESPEARE

Walkers passed me often, and most of them were keen to stop for a chat.

A group of four older people, my age, showed concern over my shuffling progress.

Before speeding off, they asked if anyone knew where I was.

Sis has found an app, called Polarsteps that plots my position.

I can't argue that I am packing carbs like Scott, before it all started to go wrong, but I also can't help but laugh at the name Polarsteps.

I imagine myself wearing sealskin and pulling a sledge heroically across the poles, not mincing on a gammy leg, begging small packets of Cathedral City and baguette and Dairy Milk from a complete stranger.

Mike, my age, from Cardiff, a serious trail walker, bore down on me from behind, carrying a huge pack full of dehydrated food and Dairy Milk.

He had spent the last evening in a hotel in Westward Ho! and was raring to go, with strong legs, and a mission to get to Rick Stein's in Padstow by next Saturday.

We greeted each other as I got caught up in his slipstream, and he slowed and suggested we walk together.

Mike was a chatty man, with a great sense of humour, whose wife abhorred walking and had gone on a beach holiday with her friends.

I told him that my husband liked walking, and by coincidence had also just been on a beach holiday with his friends.

Mike laughed conspiratorially, and suggested we should swap.

I'M NO SHAKESPEARE

I immediately got out my phone, opened my notes app, and spoke the words dramatically as I typed them.

'Mike', 'Cardiff', 'Wife swap'.

Mike looked alarmed, and I told him, with an innocent smile, that I was writing a book.

He made no further mention of swaps.

At Bucks Hills, after meeting up again with the previous group of four walkers, Mike shared his lunch with me.

The conversation between us all was interesting, centering on epigenetics and on whether exercise really makes any difference to weight.

I managed to add something to the conversation along the lines of it now taking thirteen breaths instead of seventeen to inflate my mattress.

But really all I could think about, Labrador-like, was whether Mike would offer me any more of his Dairy Milk.

After lunch the group of now five pulled ahead, and I continued alone, happily lost in my thoughts, at my snail's pace.

With each day that passed, some, like now, with barely any distinction between day and night, I felt myself slipping further and further into the delicious deep waters and the merry madness of the lone long distance walker.

I walked past an electrified fence, trying to fight the irresistible urge to touch it, 'just to see'.

Whilst simultaneously wondering if there was any way I could harness its power to charge my waning telephone battery.

I'M NO SHAKESPEARE

A lady complimented me on my "colours", which are predominantly turquoise.

I thanked her and answered, in all seriousness, that I had had my colours done in Cotswold Outdoors.

Well I am no Boris, but it is really not hard to make the public believe any old nonsense.

For the final two mile long approach to Clovelly I limped along an old carriage track that is no longer open to vehicular transport.

The Hobby drive was built between 1811 and 1829, after the Napoleonic wars, by Sir James Hamlin Williams.

When built it would have had breathtaking views of the Atlantic.

For me, not perched elegantly in a pre-Victorian carriage, the experience was one of endless trudge, with the views of the sea mostly obscured by mature trees.

So a long day, twenty kms covered in nine hours, and there I was, once more sitting outside my tent, and life was good.

I drank warm Stella, and ate cold ravioli straight out of a tin.

A tin that boasted of containing one portion of my five a day.

Your guess is as good as mine.

DAY 14

Therapeutic Gait

The cockerel started its crowing at 0500, followed by the engine sounds of the first traffic from the busy road beside which I was camped.

Then the seagulls, never to be left out of a good noise party, joined in the cacophony.

I burrowed myself deeper into my bag, aware of a further drop in air temperature, and a continuing dull and throbbing pain in my right shin.

Hauling myself back to full consciousness with the help of a slow camp breakfast of strong black coffee and porridge, I added a clotted cream substitute of paracetamol and ibuprofen.

And, for certainly not the first time in my life, I marvelled at how easily a slightly damp and unremarkable pair of supermarket extra support big pants could be fashioned into an effective medical device.

Today a compression bandage for poor old Tibialis, tomorrow who knows.

I'M NO SHAKESPEARE

My pants are certainly big enough to form an arm sling, and I am quite convinced, although fingers crossed they will never be called into action for this, that they could stem a significant blood flow.

The possibilities are limitless.

I decided that they too deserved their own lyrics.

Ode to my Pants (to the tune of "Lucille")

There's a fine line 'tween compression 'n tourniquet

With pins in my needles and a throb in my foot.

There's a fine line 'tween compression 'n tourniquet ...

I know, I am no Alexander Pushkin, but I did tell you I could write poetry.

It was a mile to walk back from Roey's Retreat campsite to the end of the Hobby Drive.

From there, just as I reached the large field gate through which I would have to pass to commence today's walk, the sky turned grey and it started to rain.

In the time it took to cover my backpack and to extract and pull on my waterproof trousers and jacket I was drenched.

I continued walking along a tree lined, muddy track, beside a field, and stopped as I saw my way ahead blocked by a cuddle of at least ten cows.

They were all staring at me, unblinkingly, like cowboys ready for a shoot out.

How should I handle this?

I'M NO SHAKESPEARE

Ha, I thought, I have poles, so I will wave them like I have seen Adam do on Country file, and make farmer noises.

Like magic the cows parted.

And then, alarmingly, they began to follow me, no doubt convinced I must be hiding real farmer cow treats in my pocket.

Something told me that whatever I did, I should not run.

So I continued to make increasingly panicked farmer noises, while executing a Weird Dutch sideways scuttle, and doing my best not to lose eye contact with the bovine beasts.

The next gate could not have come soon enough, and I made a mental note to ask my friend Belinda, who is a cow expert, about appropriate human behavior when passing through fields of cows.

The heavy rain shower soon passed, the air cleared, and the fresh colours of the sea and of the surrounding nature appeared even more vivid.

I stopped at the deserted pebble cove of Mouth Mill for a morning snack of an entire packet of Cadburys chocolate covered biscuits, glad that I hadn't had to sacrifice them to the cows.

With the creamy Super Power of Cadburys once again coursing through my veins, I started the first of several steep climbs on my way towards Hartland Point.

[Note to Agent: Sis, how many times do you think I should mention Cadburys before they send me out someone with a supply of Dairy Milk?]

Halfway along the winding, wooded path out of Mouth Mill I pulled off the track for a toilet stop, and hid behind a gnarly tree trunk.

I'M NO SHAKESPEARE

Just a few moments later, while I was still behind the tree, two Germans sped past, attacking the path as if on an Autobahn.

I remained hidden which reawakened my inner Tarzan, and I fought to repress another urge to roar.

I was pleased that I had set off, despite my painful leg.

Had I opted for another rest day, then I would not have met Gunter, the Gentle German, another through-walker, who was walking towards me from Poole.

Gunter was older than me, and had ways of making me walk.

He told me his legions, I mean legs, had also known battle with Tibialis, and that I needed to get tough.

I needed to start giving the Rotten Roman a taste of his own medicine.

Not quite the old Coliseum trick of tying one leg to one chariot, and the other leg to another, but not far off.

Apparently, there is a brutal stretch that hurts like a hornet, but which Gunter promised, on the life of his Chancellor, would work.

He dropped his pack, got down on one knee, leaned forward, and proposed.

His proposal was that I copy this movement as often as possible, to loosen Tibialis' grip of my cankles, I mean ankle to knee area.

So I invented a moving therapy, based on what Gunter had demonstrated.

My therapeutic gait.

And I practiced it regularly.

And it worked.

I'M NO SHAKESPEARE

Not completely.

Not yet.

But I could definitely feel an improvement.

My therapeutic gait would not be found in any traditional physiotherapy textbook.

It is a hybrid of a Red Square soldier and the Sugar Plum Fairy, and involves a slow backwards point of the foot, toes en pointe but in motion, for about ten steps at a time.

I was thrilled and cannot thank Gunter enough.

I had been fortunate until then, to have had only one blister.

The reason was likely to be my pace, as I never walked fast enough to build up any friction.

My specialist hiking socks had also been utterly superb.

They are called one thousand mile socks, and although already anarchically threatening to walk off on their own and to leave me barefooted if I didn't wash them by five hundred miles, I did really love them.

[Note to Agent: Sis, do you think my readers may like another Ode?]

On a steep downhill section, with not a soul in sight, I stumbled across a random shovel.

It was leaning against an undisturbed bank of fern and bracken, as if it had been placed there deliberately.

I'm no Agatha Christie, but I did start plotting how I may approach my agent with a sideways move into crime fiction.

I'M NO SHAKESPEARE

A cunning plan to avoid the Himalayan Peaks Hike, Columbian Cartel Trail, or whatever other little walk my sister may be busy "lining up".

After a superb lunch of pilchards, buttery mash, and a deliciously creamy and crunchy Cadburys Twix bar, my sister WhatsApped me once again.

She had three urgent demands:

The first: that I **MUST** send all future agent notes directly to her, so as not to interrupt my 'flow'.

The second: under **NO** circumstances should I attempt any Ode to my socks.

To her first demand I humbly agreed.

I continued to petulantly consider her second.

But I drew a hard line at her third.

No sis, I will **NOT** wear an earpiece.

It was a long walk out to Hartland Point, the last section through field after field of cut hay, with borders several meters wide deliberately left full of a colourful riot of wild flowers.

Bees, butterflies and other insects busied themselves along these borders, making it clear how important these rewilding areas were, in suburban areas as well as out here on remote farmland.

I met a man who was walking slowly and making notes on a clipboard.

I am no Miss Marple, but I did stop to ask his name and to question his motives.

I'M NO SHAKESPEARE

Tom informed me that he was performing a butterfly count, and that the trend is always down.

Year on year, even out here, there are fewer butterflies.

Heidi was seventy, radiant, and had just been skinny-dipping in a rock pool.

She was on holiday, staying alone in a youth hotel and walking sections of the path.

She restored old china and was fascinating to talk with.

We chatted for a while, overlooking the Hartland weather station, before I descended to a large hut with outside trestle benches and a welcome sign that read Tea Room.

The Tea Lady was used to coast path walkers coming through like locusts.

I ordered a ham and cheese baguette, a lemon and white chocolate muffin, and a large tea.

I took her last satsuma too, for health reasons, to supplement my trail diet of blackberries, and all things Cadbury.

She craftily upsold me a pair of soft turquoise alpaca socks and, due to so much time spent with her eating and chatting, she also sent me off with a shortcut to Stoke Barton campsite.

She clearly described a higher coastal path, over a short section of my final leg to Hartland Quay, which, she assured me, would avoid a long descent and ascent.

As time was getting on, and it was true that I had spent almost as much time eating and chatting as walking, I took her advice.

I'M NO SHAKESPEARE

After blindly following one barely defined sheep path and two overgrown Devon lanes, I finally made it to Stoke Barton Farm at 1900, after twenty one kilometers and ten hours.

It was not until returning to my tent from the toilet block, practicing my therapeutic gait as I went, that I spotted the familiar orange of the Dutchman's tent.

And a white beard disappearing behind a hastily closed zip.

DAY 15

Angels

I woke in the early hours, chilled to the bone and gasping for breath.

My merino wool thermals, down jacket, and new alpaca bed socks were no match for the plummeting night time temperature.

To escape the cold I had somehow burrowed myself further than normal into my down sleeping bag, which in turn had burrowed itself even deeper into my bivvy.

The Alpkit Hunka is a nuclear bunker of a bivvy which had now sealed itself over my head, and was refusing to allow any air flow in any direction.

My sleeping system was malfunctioning, and I was in mortal danger of both suffocation and freezing.

After some fumbling, and with great relief, I located both a breathing hole, and my phone, which I always allow to bed down close to me for what is usually my battery saving body warmth, and I considered my options.

Should I call my agent?

I'M NO SHAKESPEARE

Or perhaps the coastguard?

Should I risk further deathly chills by pulling on my waterproof layers?

Or, should I try to distract myself by moving into midnight Ode mode?

As this was clearly an emergency situation, I chose the latter.

Ode to my Socks (to the tune of Rhinestone Cowboy)

We are handsome cowboys

   Riding out in the boots

   Of a queer sweating hobo

Oh

And there's no gate or gait we can't climb,

Damp or dry we are simply sublime,

   We are handsome cowboys

Oh yeah

I remembered that I had missed my usual hot shower before bed, which was a likely contributor to my bone chilling, sleepless night, and to my later hygiene issues.

There had been a queue stretching around the barns, and I had been impatient to start cooking, and eating.

I broke camp at 0700, knowing that today's walk would be tough, perhaps the hardest of the entire South West Coast Path.

Before starting to walk, I stopped in the site's Common Room where I made coffee with extra sugar, and ate porridge, and a super nutty Cadburys Snickers bar.

I'M NO SHAKESPEARE

A older lady came to join me.

Dorothy was an English teacher, and a cold water swimmer from Oxford, and she was a complete delight to converse with.

I am almost convinced that cold water swimming affords its buoy pulling practitioners entry to a portal through which they may enter a state of total transcendence.

My theory at least held true with Dorothy, until our conversation was stopped in its tracks by an older male.

He entered the room, delighted to have a female audience.

Then, with Dorothy winking and eye rolling at me like a Punch and Judy puppet, he began an endless explanation of the workings of the kettle, Catherine Cookson novels, his travels in Turkey in the 1970's where he was almost arrested for political espionage, and his fears of having breathed in deadly nuclear dust as he once flew over Chernobyl just after the meltdown.

Dorothy and I stood together like rabbits in headlights, and eventually I managed to mention my Odes.

I had hoped to impress her as she was a real English teacher, and I sensed she may understand.

She blinked, and appeared confused, then nodded, regained her composure, and looked at her watch.

Mandy was a year one teacher from Manchester.

Her husband was working, but she was out alone having a youth hostelling and coast path holiday in Devon and Cornwall, and walking a section at a time.

She said it was to get away from children.

I'M NO SHAKESPEARE

Mandy walked past me not long after I had rejoined the path.

I was sitting on a flat rock at its edge and prepping my blister, which required some more fluid removal.

I was very excited, after only having used its bottle opening gadget on my Stella at Clovelly, to play for the second time with my fantastic new thirteen function Swiss Army penknife.

I pre-warned her that I was about to perform surgery, and that she might want to look away, but Mandy was tough.

She was from Manchester, and was used to six year olds grazes, gashes, and gang warfare.

My hurty toe and mere one inch blade did not impress her at all.

So, as I released another gob of pus, we continued chatting and compared our off duty teacher faces.

The ones that we use to scare off children who come too close when we are out of working hours, or on aeroplanes.

In my determination to keep the sea firmly on my right, within constant sight, and to ignore any well-meaning advice to the contrary, I somehow veered left.

Finding myself heading up an inland valley I extracted my telephone from my fanny pack.

There was no signal, but I managed to find a small hamlet, later identified as Milford.

Instinctively I thought I was heading back towards the coast, but my instincts cannot always be trusted.

I'M NO SHAKESPEARE

So when I saw Brian in his garden holding a strimmer, I felt I may have located a rare local inhabitant of the village.

"Hello" I said.

"I am a wayward and gone wrong Coast Path walker".

Brian, in his seventies, slowly lowered his strimmer, raised an eyebrow, and looked me up and down, hand on hip.

"I can see all that", he Devon drawled, like Clint Eastwood.

I suddenly felt shy.

I asked him if he may please point me in the right direction to a bridleway or a footpath, or a long lost Devon lane that might get me back on track to Morwenstow.

He suggested he walk with me, probably to see me safely out of his village, but I was thrilled to have longer to chat with him.

Brian was actually a Yorkshire man but had lived in Devon for forty years where he had worked "on the wires" as a telephone engineer.

After retirement, and with both he and his wife suffering from medical ailments not responding to the usual GP led care, they had headed to a healing centre in Bude.

They had both recovered well after their healing sessions, and subsequently decided to attend the six month training course to attain their own Healer qualifications.

Interestingly, all those on the course also passed.

Brian explained how he attracts clients and then either treats them at their homes or takes them to the healing clinic.

"It's quite easy" he said.

I'M NO SHAKESPEARE

"Anyone could do it if they learned how"

I was amazed, and asked if he would be so kind as to heal my blister and the traitorous Tibialis.

I reassured him that he would not need to actually touch my foot.

"Oh that's perfectly fine" he replied.

"I don't have to touch to heal."

"I can even do it by email and have several clients from the USA".

I tried to keep a straight face because Brian really was very nice and kind, and great fun to chat to.

He told me that he also performed Angel Healing, of which I knew nothing.

He explained that there are Angels all around us, and that he asks them for their healing help.

Their energy then transfers itself with tingles and heat to his palms.

I was transfixed, and wanted to ask if the Angel's numbers were also on the decline, like the butterflies.

We reached the edge of a gated field, and Brian explained that I would need to climb over the gate, walk across the field, and then climb over a second gate which borders the path.

We shook hands and parted amicably.

My head still full of Angel questions, I threw my pack and poles over the second gate, relieved to finally be back on track.

I'M NO SHAKESPEARE

As I was straddling the top rung of the gate, I looked down into the smiling blue eyes of another hiker.

Peter was Polish, slightly younger than me, and offered me his hand with no thought to where mine may have been.

I took his hand gratefully and with a similar ignorance, seduced by his smile and his hard Slavic accent.

He told me he had just come from Tinder Girl, which, due to his swagger, I had no trouble believing.

It turned out, however, that he had meant Tintagel.

I giggled, thanked him for his European chivalry, and we waved goodbye.

After a couple of kms I started at the sight, a few steps ahead of me, of a beautiful new model Stobart, shiny, with young undented bodywork.

It had shed its load and was lying, eyes closed and motionless, jackknifed, with boots half blocking the path.

Oh my goodness, or something similar, I thought, as my twenty years of working front line in the ambulance service come flooding back to me.

Could there be an impending ambush, or a nest of rattlesnakes?

Should I shout, or just kick him, to check if he is conscious?

And then, out loud, as if in a training scenario, I ran through my next steps.

"Is his airway clear?"

"Is he breathing?"

"Does he have a pulse?"

I'M NO SHAKESPEARE

"Commence chest compressions'

(At the point where your crew mate calls for back up and sets up the defibrillator, I did, very briefly, reconsider an earpiece).

The corners of the young casualty's mouth began to tremble, and his chest spasmed, as he started what I feared may be a seizure.

But thankfully not.

Just laughter.

The rib breaking laughter that I have come to recognize as the unique laughter of the lone long distance hiker.

I laughed with him, and apologised for my intrusion.

Then I continued, as yet oblivious to the reason for his exhaustion, but soon to find out ...

The next section of the path was brutal and, from the sea, the coastline must look like a crocodile's mandible.

As I arose from the steep ascent out of each cove I could already see the next descents waiting for me.

The rain set in and I soon became very wet.

Initially the wind had been almost non-existent, and I had remembered my hiking umbrella.

I had attached it expertly to the redundant ice axe fitting on my backpack, tying its velcro fastener to the opposite side of my Tilley hat strap.

It had worked a treat and I carried on smugly, resembling a dishevelled and ill-refined Edwardian lady.

I'M NO SHAKESPEARE

Until the wind got up, whereupon I struggled to untie the double granny knot that was holding an inside out brolly on my head.

I raced against time to disentangle myself before a gust of wind may have carried me, like Mary Poppins, off the cliffs.

After summiting a particularly steep stepped cliff I arrived at a bench, sheltered on three sides by bilberry bushes.

I rested there awhile to regain my breath, and boiled a pot of water to which I added an entire packet of buttery mashed potato powder, and a tin of pilchards.

I'm no Rick Stein, but it was the most delicious fish based meal humanly possibly to prepare.

If you are reading this, Rick, then I will give you the actual recipe when I pass through Padstow next week.

I really like you.

And I really like fish and chips.

And mushy peas.

Tucked under the brow of one such descent, my feet swimming inside my boots, and a damp chill beginning to take hold, I came across the Ronald Duncan shelter.

The shelter is a stone built, one roomed, bothy, with three narrow wooden benches, a table upon which rests a visitor book and a biro, and walls with posters to tell the tale of the local poet and playwright to whom this shelter is dedicated.

There are examples of his work, and that of other poets, displayed on the walls.

I'M NO SHAKESPEARE

I studied them all, and this poem by John Moat was my favourite:

Welcome Beach

The pebbles are out of order. Some man's
> been down to meddle with the stones again.
> On the wide mindless beach this one thought
> Breaks out to spoil the sea's unthinkable design.
> He's been building, stone lifted onto stone
> No one else on the beach, he builds a fort -
> To live with himself. Sandcastles and forts
> And wailing walls and burial mounds - and then
> At sundown, after the last man has gone
> From the shore, the sea moves in without a thought
> And smooths the beach. And now the builder has gone
> And the patient sea is on the move again.
> It smooths the pebbles into place, and the thought
> Falls into place. And I, the last thought standing alone,
> Am drawn to the peace that will follow when I too have gone.

In the shelter of the hut, before heading off again, I swapped my sodden socks for my second less wet pair, and put on my dry, merino wool pyjama top as an extra layer.

I added my signature to the visitor's book, and felt the frisson of my first book signing.

I'M NO SHAKESPEARE

I decided however, against adding an Ode of my own.

I'm no Vladimir Putin, but do know I can sometimes be a bit deluded.

The remainder of the walk, from the hut to my refuge for the night, in a small hedged-in slug garden behind the garden and wooden children's play area of the Bush Inn in Morwenstow, was strenuous.

The weather worsened and I was alone on the headlands with no other mortals, Angels, phone signal, or indeed any distractions other than my own at times somewhat disturbing thoughts.

It was deep at the bottom of another ravine, as I was beginning to feel the benefit of the warm insulation of my third base layer, when by chance I looked up to see the Cornwall/Kernow border crossing point.

A simple wooden sign, and no visa required.

As I began to ascend again, the unique molecules of my natural body aroma began to escape, silently, from the neck of my waterproof jacket.

A heady blend of deep ocean trench, and camel scrotum.

Yesterday my turquoise buff had decided to walk off a cliff, and I was beginning to understand why.

Empathising with its despair, but not quite yet feeling the need to be quite so attention seeking, I removed my new turquoise bed socks from my pack and stuffed them firmly down my decollete.

The recoiling tang of unwashed bodies wearing long unwashed clothes, earth and pavement dirt mingling only too often with stale

I'M NO SHAKESPEARE

cigarette smoke and the sweetness of drug use, is unmistakable to me.

In my non-path world, where I took daily showers and had instant access to a washing machine, I would never have believed it possible for my own body to produce the stench of street living within only a few days.

I should have had more compassion during my years in the ambulance service.

Finally, I saw an inland church spire, and I recalled how my Grandad, who had always enjoyed a lunchtime pint and game of darts at the Cock inn in Headley, Surrey, would have said that where there is a church there is a pub.

They go together like fish and chips, salt and pepper, or, well, Mary and Jesus.

Before long, just one weary and wary crossing of a cow field later, a voluminously breasted middle aged woman stood damply at the bar in the Bush Inn in Morwenstow, and asked for grass.

The barman lifted his gaze, grinned, and pointed to the small area of the pub garden that was reserved for walkers, who may camp there for free if they buy a meal.

After setting up a sodden tent in the wind and rain, and after preparing my sleeping bag and belongings for a grand prix tyre change of a bedtime routine, I returned gratefully to the bar where I ordered the first of two pints of Tribute, and attempted to get dry.

A granite inglenook fireplace was loaded with logs but, because "we do not light it until the Autumn" it remained only as a teasing still life.

I'M NO SHAKESPEARE

I ordered an enormous peppercorn steak, with salad and chips; and, because it was so totally impossible to choose between them, two puddings.

DAY 16

Civilization

It had been clearly explained to me the previous evening that breakfast at the Inn was only offered to guests who were staying in the guest rooms upstairs.

My request, for any leftover sausages to possibly please be thrown over the hedge into the slug mating garden, had been refused.

Apparently, the landlords prefer to keep a healthy separation between the foul smelling freebie campers and their fragrant ensuite paying guests.

Fair enough really.

They do have a point, although I am not sure Wetherspoons would have been so picky.

I really was very cold, and the rain had prevented me from lighting my stove beside my tent.

So at 0730 I slunk guiltily into the pub's flagstone floored accessible toilet, where I warmed myself up by boiling water for coffee, and porridge, with a soupçon of pilchard.

I'M NO SHAKESPEARE

I walked back to the coast path through the thick morning mist mixed with the warm breath of cattle, and I hugged the hedge perimeter to hide from cows, and to not miss the field gate.

My view was perfectly framed by the brim of my Tilly hat and the sides of the hood of my waterproof coat.

I recalled myself as a teenager, shy and self-conscious, hiding from the world and picking my spots.

My favourite coat at that time, was the in fashion Snorkel parka.

It boasted a hood that once fully zipped gave its wearer the appearance of a surfacing submarine.

My tastes have never since collided with modern fashion.

Except possibly for last week, when the straggliest boy at the end of the last straggling group of boys on a Duke of Edinburgh cliff top expedition had complimented me loudly as he straggled past, "Loving your Crocs!".

The coastline was again captivating, with many steep sided coves to be traversed.

The sea boiled far below me, and in the cove bottoms the whoosh and pull of powerful waves hitting the jagged dark rocked cliffs echoed loudly.

Not even the discomfort of my wet socks could dampen my wide smile at being witness to such incredible beauty.

Descending into Stanbury Mouth I gazed across the valley towards another stairway to hell that ascended to the next headland.

How marvellous, I thought.

I'M NO SHAKESPEARE

The perfect moment to break open my huge bar of Cadburys Dairy milk with delicately crushed hazelnuts which I had panic purchased at the bar last night, after hearing the disappointing news that I would be refused a traditional breakfast.

I rested for a while, and ate, brazenly ignoring the wrapper instructions to "Open and Reclose", and opting instead for "Open, Eat, Lick Wrapper, and Dispose".

Another good news story was that Tibialis had now left Britannica for the Eternal City, via Gaul I supposed, to torment the French.

With the creative juice suppressing pain now lifted, I was once again called towards my poetry.

Reclining on a hard slab of stone I observed my beaker, hanging limply, forlornly, from another as yet unidentified attachment loop on my pack.

I was overcome with compassion for this much overlooked kit member, which two days ago had come to the rescue of Thomas, a thirsty Rottweiler, by providing a perfectly sized water receptacle for his tongue.

I felt it deserved its own Ode.

Ode to my Beaker: (To the tune of "Don't Cry for Me, Argentina"

Don't cry for me, I'm a Beaker

    I have a hard life,

    And don't I know it.

    I'm used for coffee

I'M NO SHAKESPEARE

A drooly Rotty

A midnight po - o - tty ...

In Duckpool, a remote cove but one where a road leads to a beach car park, Jenny was sitting on a simple folding beach chair behind her pride and joy.

She and her husband had met as young travellers in Amsterdam, before continuing to New Zealand and settling happily there.

Jenny and her family had later returned to the UK for personal reasons, but swerved returning to her home town of Peterborough for the dramatic North Devon coast.

A place that reminded her of her home in New Zealand.

Jenny now runs her own business called Hedgerows, selling extremely decent coffee, tea, and cake from another beautifully logoed small van.

The back doors of her van were open, providing an exceptional three sided windbreak, and displaying a shining barista station.

In the fresh air of the cove, Jenny reads novels in between waiting for customers, and she appears to have found the perfect work life balance.

We chatted, I ordered coffee with coffee cake, and she lent me her chair.

I moved considerately downwind, so that I could squeeze water out of my socks and allow my feet to share in some of this intoxicating freedom.

After scaling several more crocodile teeth I stopped at a cafe in Sandymouth, where I sat for an hour with more coffee and cake,

I'M NO SHAKESPEARE

finally savouring the pleasure of warmth and dryness, and allowing time for my phone to charge.

In Bude I rested once again on a bench, inscribed with a line of another beautiful poem by Alfred Lord Tennyson called Crossing the Bar, which was written in 1889 three years before his death.

It is a poem that I had heard read only a month previously, at a funeral

Crossing the Bar

Sunset and evening star

    And one clear call for me!

    And may there be no moaning of the bar,

    When I put out to sea,

    But such a tide as moving seems asleep,

    Too full for sound and foam,

    When that which drew from out the boundless deep

    Turns again home.

    Twilight and evening bell,

    And after that the dark!

    And may there be no sadness of farewell,

    When I embark;

    For tho' from out our bourne of Time and Place

    The flood may bear me far,

    I hope to see my Pilot face to face When I have crost the bar.

I'M NO SHAKESPEARE

The words of the poem seemed more poignant as I observed coast guard officers, wearing full rescue equipment, carefully and urgently scanning the rough sea through binoculars.

Sheila was walking through the car park in Bude.

She had a kind and open expression, and was wearing a simple woollen jumper in a beautiful shade of pink.

My attention was drawn to her hand crafted spiralled willow walking pole.

We smiled at each other as we passed and I stopped to ask about the pole.

We chatted and she enjoyed telling me that her brother designs walking poles by tying twine tightly around willow, in a spiral.

The twine then directs the subsequent willow growth to follow the spiral pattern.

For thirty years Sheila had been returning to Bude for her holidays.

She told me proudly that she was now the matriarch of four generations of her family who had grown up holidaying in Bude, and she kindly allowed me to photograph her with her brother's unique walking pole.

I left Sheila to continue walking into the busy shopping centre where I purchased a new gas cylinder.

I then used my telephone to navigate a short distance further to a central but simple field campsite, with a basic portacabin washroom.

That evening, very soon, from the strange land of civilization, I would be joined by my friend Helen.

I'M NO SHAKESPEARE

Irrepressible Helen.

Scuba Dive Master and fellow midnight skinny dipper Helen.

She was keen to camp and walk with me for four nights and would be bringing her rain hating dog, Django, and her new tent.

I was resting in my sleeping bag, a calm before the approaching social storm, preparing myself for some nose wrinkling from Helen, and perhaps some interesting canine sniffing from Django.

When I am on the path I have a rule, that if I think about doing something, I immediately do it.

For example, if I think I need to drink water, I drink water.

If I think I need to rest, I rest.

The same with taking off or putting on a layer of clothing, or a hat, applying sunscreen, removing grit from my socks, or tightening a shoelace.

It is an effective way to keep self discipline and it helps me to stay safe.

My brain was given a firm shake, and I warned it that it must not, under any circumstances, attempt any 'if you think it, just say it'.

DAY 17

Sauna

The night was finally a dry and calm one, with none of the recent albatross caught in the rigging nonsense.

Immediately upon their arrival, Helen and her partner, having hurled horrified looks at me, decided I needed a good meal.

I was in fact still swimming in coffee and cake, but was too polite to turn down a free meal, and a couple pints of Tribute.

My usual no nonsense morning routine was slightly extended by Helen's superior hygiene, by her Garmin issues, and by her completely reasonable emotional trepidation to walking with me.

Helen had been utterly unaware of my current mental state, and was clearly perturbed by my preponderance to cackling and breaking into songs with no meanings or tune.

Just random words, usually only vaguely recognisable, based loosely on an Elvis classic, or a Christmas Carol.

To me the social intrusion into the perfect pottiness of my lone hiker bubble was psychologically fascinating, and brought me

I'M NO SHAKESPEARE

starkly face to face with the depth of my current lunatic reality, as viewed through the eyes of an office worker.

All of that notwithstanding, we enjoyed an epic day, sharing secrets, taking a spontaneous beach sauna, sea swimming in our underwear, and tandem wild weeing.

Bude to Crackington Haven is as tough as any section from Hartland to Bude.

Steep valleys and steps, and several fields of cows, one after the other after the other.

We arrived at a pub in Crackington Haven at 20:00, from where we were collected by a kind campsite owner.

She drove us, and Django, inland to her campsite, where after a rehydrated, dehydrated dinner, we simply collapsed into our respective tents.

In total physical, mental, and for me social exhaustion.

Ode to My Tilly Hat (To the tune of "Horse With No Name")

I rode through Devon on a head with no brain.

It felt bad, but there wasn't much pain.

Now riding through Cornwall,

and not much has changed

La la... la la la la …

DAY 18

Sloe Gin

Lorna used to live in Brighton where she had worked in corporate retail.

There, while her career was steadily sapping her spirit, she witnessed the rising popularity of beach saunas.

Lorna bravely decided to start her own business, introducing the concept of beach saunas to Cornwall.

Her first sauna arrived on a huge lorry, fully assembled, from Lithuania.

We met Lorna yesterday in Widemouth Bay, and it was there, in her beautiful gypsy wagon Ocean Soul Sauna, with a picture window overlooking the beach, that Helen and I ran squealing between the sauna's deep heat therapy and cold sea swimming.

Lorna kept a friendly eye on Django and on our backpacks, while, after three weeks of no decent hot showers, I realised that I had much in common with a python.

Catherine was eighty six and was from Bude.

I'M NO SHAKESPEARE

She had been the daughter of a farmer, and in 1956 she had become the wife of another farmer, from the hamlet near Crackington Haven, where we had camped the previous evening.

Catherine, who had lived there all her life, was walking her dog in the lanes at 0830 at the very same time as I was attempting to navigate us back across farmland to the Coast Path.

Django, who was wearing his raincoat and who had given up trying to herd us, was walking behind me, nose down, resignedly.

We were followed by Helen, who was hauling the kitchen sink.

I complimented Catherine on her beautiful, antique, hand knitted hat with its rose applique.

With uncanny prediction she smiled, and replied:

"Everything comes full circle, dear!"

After leading us all on a double circumnavigation of an industrial barn, and a shallow wade through a slurry pit, my synapses were momentarily cauterised by an electric cow fence.

I reminded myself to complete an extra inspection for exit wounds during tonight's check for ticks.

I sensed that my friend was beginning to enjoy sharing my world.

Helen, who for context has not long returned from diving with sharks in the Red Sea, and who has little to no concept of fear, had been recounting the tale of the Pembrokeshire Coast Path murders.

Apparently her uncle, who at that time was the local GP in Newport, was arrested and questioned by the local police in relation to the incidents.

I'M NO SHAKESPEARE

Although subsequently found to be entirely innocent, he had fitted the suspect's description of:

"Curly, blond hair and a beard".

You can therefore imagine my own imaginings when, from the opposite side of a steep valley, we saw a man of the exact same description, running quickly and determinedly in our direction.

Helen was unflinching.

But I, in our few remaining moments before certain death, considered my options.

For obvious reasons turning and running in the opposite direction was immediately ruled out.

An implementation of our really quite brutal 'only to be used in the event of killer cows' pre-planned, emergency four-pronged pole attack was perhaps a bit premature.

We had agreed that the pole attack was only to be initiated as an absolute last resort, instantly, upon the secret password signal being shouted, and only when one hundred percent certain of threat status.

Kevin, forty six today, was running to Crackington Haven, like he does every year on his birthday.

He was listening to his favourite music through his air pods and was lost in his own thoughts.

He was completely unaware of the furore ahead of him.

Nor was he aware that he was about to be held in conversation with a Tilly hat wearing middle aged woman, with just two aims: to make him feel more terrified than her, and to make him think that she was more dangerous than him.

I'M NO SHAKESPEARE

"Hello! Tell me what you gain from running?"

"Um, well it's my birthday and I'm running to Crackington Haven"

"What, for beer and birthday cake?"

"Um, no, for fitness"

"We have been making sloe gin while we walk.

Wild sloes, mixed with night time urine and half chewed Haribos.

Would you like to try some?"

The strategy worked surprisingly well, and Helen and I laughed so much that I asked her if she could perhaps take a further few days off work, to continue walking with me.

She hesitated, picked up her dog, and mumbled something about needing to return for a performance review.

I am really no Conservative, but I do sometimes find it hard to know when I am being fibbed to.

Ode to my Stove (To the tune of 'Jolene')

Baked beans, baked beans, baked beans, baked beans

    I'm begging of you please don't hurt my pan

    With ignition beyond compare

    And flames of butane gas I swear,

    I really, really, really love my pan ...

DAY 19

Wild Camp

After a pub dinner in Boscastle, and an impromptu karaoke with some local men on a Saturday night out, we pitched on the cliff top, in gusting wind, just before the rain started.

We were at a Caravan Club site with excellent level facilities and a fabulous shower block for caravans.

As campers, however, we were told we must pitch on a sloping field with its own portaloos.

The white noise of the sea, wind and rain, in combination with the body heat generated by the challenge of having been wrestling to pin down sheets of feral nylon, afforded warm and restful sleep.

As always, I was incredulous of the stability and waterproof qualities of my tent.

The day's planned hike to Port Isaac was described in the book as follows:

"The first half of the walk, from Tintagel to Trebarwith Strand, has several short ascents and descents, but these aren't too difficult.

I'M NO SHAKESPEARE

The second half of the walk features an arduous series of steep ascents and descents to Port Isaac."

At 0800, we were still cocooned in our respective shelters, listening to the continuing symphony of white noise.

A mutual decision, reached through blindly shouting in the direction of each other's tents, was made.

To enjoy a little longer in bed.

Perhaps, after coffee and porridge, and if there were a break in the rain showers, we may consider a short stroll to Trebarwith Strand.

For a pasty and a sea swim.

Eventually, following a consensus to count to three and to do a synchronized unzip, we opened up our tents, took one at our respective ghastliness, and screamed.

It was decided that we both urgently required a shower, so we headed off on a mission to infiltrate the Caravan Club stone built and centrally heated shower facilities.

What a luxury it was!

Piping hot water without having to hold your bottom awkwardly against cold steel faucets, and a powerful hair dryer with which we blasted dry not only our hair, but our socks and walking boots.

The sea was wild, too rough even for surfers, and we walked carefully along the rugged, slate coast, witnessing the evidence of old slate quarries.

We stopped at Tintagel, which was crowded with day visitors, to enjoy the excellent National Trust coffee, cake, and toilet facilities.

I'M NO SHAKESPEARE

It was a Sunday and our late afternoon and evening were spent anchored to armchairs in the luxury of the Trebarwith Strand Inn, where we ate a delicious roast dinner, and drank several cold beers.

Django was fed well, thanks to a jar of complimentary dog treats, and we fully charged our electronic devices.

At 1930 we left, reluctantly, to begin the merry climb of the two hundred steep cliff steps out of the cove.

Crossing a grassy field and descending steeply into a rough coastal valley, we spotted the perfect wild camping area, in the remains of a ruined slate mining building at the edge of the cliff.

Two partial walls were all that were still standing, behind which we made our camp, just before the rain once again arrived.

DAY 20

Cryptosporidium

It was an alarming night, with our sleep severely interrupted by strong, gusting wind.

All my possessions were pulled into my inner sanctum, in case the worst were to occur and my tarp be ripped free.

In fact the double pegging and placement of heavy slate rocks on top of all pegged areas meant that all remained intact, and my confidence in my tent was further increased.

At 0730, with the wind speed finally beginning to decrease, I unzipped to witness the enormous power and beauty of the waves crashing once more into the tiny rocky cove above which we were camped.

To the distinctive call of a Peregrine Falcon that was nesting in the slate cliff directly above us I lit my stove.

Qigong beside my tent afforded release from last night's tense, coiled spring-like, non-sleeping position, and a fellow Coast Path walker, passing at a rate of knots, waved a cheery hello.

I'M NO SHAKESPEARE

Most wild campers pitch late, just before dark, and set off again at dawn.

We took our time, breakfasted magnificently on tuna pasta salad and Mars Bars, and left, in the rain, to continue an even more strenuous and challenging walk towards Port Gaverne.

The weather forecast once again predicted a week of wet weather, with particularly strong wind for the following day.

Walking downhill on slippery mud and slate was especially difficult, and we made slow progress with several trips.

Long wet grass overhanging the narrow paths caused water to fill our boots, which further soaked our already damp socks.

We saw very few other walkers as we trudged onwards, but stopped to watch, from our vantage point high above a remote sandy beach, as a lone female skipped towards the sea, and entered the breaking waves.

Her single set of footprints was only just visible to us from our elevated cliff top lookout.

We observed her body language as she jumped, wetsuit free, through the initial shock of the cold waves, appearing as happy as a puppy in a puddle.

So, with a personal rebrand to happy as hippos in a muddy river, we smiled, high-fived, and continued stumbling onwards, to our first stop at a sheltered, but even muddier spot, where we boiled water for hot chocolate.

A four minute rolling boil, because we had run out of water, and so had risked collecting stream water.

Helen works for South West Water as a Pollution Technician.

I'M NO SHAKESPEARE

Therefore, with fingers firmly crossed behind my back, and in the knowledge that my medicine bag contained both activated charcoal and imodium, I trusted her advice.

As we had only one remaining sachet of hot chocolate, we supplemented it by sharing a family sized bar of Dairy Milk, and savouring the hot, mouth melting sweetness of each half dunked chunk.

At the threshold of the Port Gaverne Inn, a droopy trio of dripping muddiness, the maitre d' stood bigly before us, blocking our way, and respectfully requested boots to be removed before entering.

Over beer and crisps we regained our strength and humour, and debriefed on our long weekend of growing old disgracefully.

Helen's partner arrived to collect her and Django, and I walked on alone to a small camping meadow.

There, for five pounds per night, with a toilet, and a one pound slot meter shower, I set up my tent.

My intention was to stay and to rest for three nights, and to allow the worst of the predicted rain storm to pass.

It had been nine days of continuous walking since I had last had a rest day.

In the knowledge that Helen would be joining me, I had pushed on further than I should have, delaying a sensible rest break.

Hunting dogs were bred opposite the camping meadow, and I listened to their strangulated barking all night, as they strained against their leashes to get at the night time rabbits.

DAY 21

Linda

By dawn all was peaceful, and the only sound I heard was the babble from the stream behind my tent.

It was the first of August and some Summer sunshine would have been welcomed.

The constant rain showers provided little reliable opportunity to deal with my laundry.

I had found an app for a nationwide immediate laundry collection and delivery service.

It was a home working initiative for which I would have been prepared to pay well.

Alas, it appeared there was no coverage for this area.

I supposed there was more money, and certainly more satisfaction, to be found in servicing second homes and Airbnb's.

And, to be quite frank, I did not want to touch my underwear either.

I'M NO SHAKESPEARE

Linda had a huge German caravan permanently parked on the site, which boasted a large awning, with a bunting and pixie filled garden.

It was a quirky little place, and I felt quite at home there.

Linda was about my age, kind, efficient, and similarly forthright, and handed me a pound coin for the shower, and some Clarins products, to "tidy yourself up".

Emboldened, I decided while I was at it to pluck at my most roguish, visible without a magnifying mirror, chin hairs.

The next morning Linda kindly popped around to check that I had at least brushed my hair.

I had not, but I had cleaned my teeth, as evidenced by the toothpaste dribbling down my chin.

Linda had also brought a plastic garden chair, telling me it would be "better for your posture than laying around in a tent".

I could not disagree, it was an absolute luxury to have furniture and I was very grateful to my new friend.

In my mid to late teens, I had emerged, snail-like, from my Snorkel Parka.

In the time before the Internet my curiosity and desire to travel had been fed by hours of standing in the travel section of book shops.

Cover to cover, I would read such books as "Work Your Way Around The World", with no means to actually purchase these books, let alone to actually reach any other country in the world.

So I set about finding as much paid work as I could fit in with my sixth form studies.

I'M NO SHAKESPEARE

My first tent and sleeping bag were bought with my wages from three separate weekend jobs.

On Saturday and Sunday mornings I would cycle to work as a chambermaid at a local Novotel.

On Friday and Saturday nights I was a cashier and server at a local fish and chip shop, and on Sundays I worked as a lunchtime pub chef.

In those days, my parents ran a residential home where I would also occasionally earn extra wages through working week day sleep-in night shifts

On the day after my last A level I travelled to New York, having secured work upstate on a Summer Camp for adults with disabilities.

Both my studies and my travelling were curtailed soon afterwards, by early marriage and the birth of my daughter.

I was just twenty, the same age my mother had been when she had given birth to me.

My first son was born two years later, and motherhood, especially single motherhood, was exciting and fulfilling.

Immediately after divorce, I was able to put every spare penny towards driving lessons, passing my test on my first try, and I was helped by my mother to buy my first car, a Mini Clubman Estate.

On the day after purchase I had baby and child seats professionally fitted, and very soon after that the three of us set off on a camping road trip into Cornwall, where we all slept together in a dome tent, full of laughter and silliness.

The children would sit excitedly, wrapped in fleece dressing gowns, after having all returned from the shower block.

I'M NO SHAKESPEARE

While little legs dangled at the back of the Mini, with both its rear doors opened wide, I would prepare hot chocolate for us on my tiny stove.

Walking through Tintagel, thirty four years later, and seeing King Arthur's Castle again, was a reminder of that magical road trip.

Were other young parents also telling their wide eyed children tales of Merlin and the Knights of the Round Table, Swords and Scabbards.

I woke, warm and paralysed, as if drugged, after a three hour deep and dream filled afternoon sleep.

Alarming yellow weather warnings for the next day were starting to pop up on my telephone, and I was delighted to be staying put.

Close enough to the path to be able to easily get going again, but well hidden, in a sheltered valley behind the headland.

Assertively insisting, against their protestations, in giving my legs a small stretch, I wandered the short distance down the lane to the Port Gaverne Inn.

Once there, I made one beer last long enough to fully charge my telephone, and enjoyed the comfortable surroundings.

As the light began to fade, a lit candle was placed on my table.

It felt romantic, and far preferable to sitting in a chilly, stark shower room waiting for my Bulgarian two pin charger to complete its slow trickle through a shaver socket.

The beach in Port Gaverne is at the end of a long narrow inlet, sheltered, and home to several small wooden fishing boats.

I'M NO SHAKESPEARE

I walked down to watch a few hardy women still swimming under thundery dark evening clouds.

Light storm precursor rain began shooting dimples over the black surface of the water, and I was tempted to join the bathing belles.

Instead I removed only my shoes, my socks, and my artisan patchwork of plasters, in various states of decomposition, and allowed my feet the healing pleasure of a salty bathe.

One blistered area on my left heel was particularly sore and was the one I was keeping the closest watch on.

It was at moderate risk of developing a deep infection, and I gently massaged it with Savlon before redressing.

The rain increased, and it took me very little deliberation before deciding to return to the Inn for my dinner.

The menu was fitting for an Inn that charges one hundred and seventy eight pounds per night for a room, and five pounds forty for a pint of Tribute, and I ordered a 'snack while you wait' of Liver Pate parfait, plus a side each of Fiery Fries and of Baby Gem Caesar.

If it had not been raining then a home cooked rehydrated dehydrated meal would have been my fine dining decision.

Dining at the Inn was a total extravagance, but I was far too easily seduced by a flickering flame, and by a deconstructed Spork.

DAY 22

Why?

I did not want to stop walking.

I did not want to deliberately cut my dream short.

I was proud to have come so far, and in such challenging, unseasonable weather.

I was proud of my kit.

And if not then, then when?

Assuming health and happiness, some people dream of obtaining degrees, of achieving qualifications.

Some people dream of love, of finding the perfect partner.

Some dream of wealth, of corporate success and ladder climbing.

Or of material things.

My dream, at that moment, was really quite modest.

I just wanted to walk a bit further.

And if not then, then when?

I'M NO SHAKESPEARE

Heavy rain had started pounding my home during the night.

In the morning, during a brief respite from the showers, I had managed to boil my water.

After breakfast I had once again fully re-zipped myself into both my tent and my sleeping bag.

The dampness of such constant rain was all pervading, and only my own body heat was keeping the worst of the damp from my clothes and sleeping bag.

This would continue only if I stayed that way, keeping away from touching the sides of my tent, and making toilet trips as brief as possible.

But another day to fully rest my leg was welcome.

I had a hot five minute shower to look forward to, and could prepare hot food and drink.

Charging facilities were basic, but dry.

I imagined how these conditions must appear to others, and the perfectly sane question that I was often asked:

"Why?"

It was impossible to provide a definitive answer, because some things are simply felt, and cannot be adequately described.

Feelings that I know are wordlessly understood by those who just know, and who would never think of asking why.

But I had time, hiding from the storm, to attempt, in as few words as possible, to answer.

I was walking for myself, for my own physical and mental challenge, and for my own self-learning and satisfaction.

I'M NO SHAKESPEARE

Walking had given my mind time and space to just settle, and to peacefully unravel its own knots.

It was a privilege to be able to witness with all my senses the breathtaking beauty of our coastline, and to be alone in remote areas between towns, with just the native flora and fauna.

To sit in stunted oak forests and inaccessible coves, and to gaze out at miles of uninterrupted sand, to sea, to horizon.

I had discovered, in my fellow long distance trail walkers, an instant camaraderie and spirit of optimism.

I loved their problem solving mentality, their eagerness to help and to support.

These are people who do not admit defeat, who never wallow in self pity, and who laugh at calamities that may bring others to tears.

Laughter truly is the best medicine.

Ode to my Odour (To the tune of 'Coward of the County')

I promised my bum, not to be that kind of mum,

   To turn away from bubbles, for a can,

   But when it's been a week, with no shower so to speak,

   The odour's rough enough to kill a man ...

In the early evening I walked once more along the lane to the cove.

I spread my arms wide for balance, trying to stay upright in the strong gusting wind, and my mental cobwebs were blown fully away.

I'M NO SHAKESPEARE

White horses were visible as far as the horizon, and waves charged furiously at the shore, noisily and frothily disturbing the peace of pebbles and sand, and depositing another trove of rounded sea glass treasure for children to discover.

I had watched the sea in many states over the past few weeks.

Sometimes it breathed sweetly, the barely visible, gentle, swelling breath of a sleeping baby.

At other times, like today, deep sobbing breaths were caught, held angrily, then explosively released with pounding tantruming fists against its shore's sore shoulders.

In English, although the sea has no gender, it is traditionally believed that something as open, mysterious, chaotic, and dangerous as the ocean is associated with the feminine.

Something or someone who has power over those things, can bring order, calm and safety, is associated with the masculine.

I am not sure that the wild spirits of the sea, or of women, have ever been truly tamed by any man.

But I do always appreciate order, calm, and safety.

In fact, a fair chunk of my female life has been spent trying to bring order to the chaos created by men and boys.

A chaos, which to be fair, would not have existed had it not been for my own lunatic hormones.

How thrilling it was to be fifty six, and to have only to deal with the chaos of the inside of my own tent

I had been thirty five when I married John in Kingsbridge town hall.

I'M NO SHAKESPEARE

Our son James, was six months old, barefooted, and was passed around all day between his six older siblings, grandparents and great grandparents.

His baby toes had spread in delight as they had fed him chocolate cake behind my back.

John dreamed of skiing, and followed his dream, after retirement, by qualifying in Bulgaria as a ski instructor.

From the UK, I had encouraged and supported him, translating his training manual, and working his shifts as well as my own.

Now he was supporting me, by sending selfies of him eating delicious Balkan meals, and reclining in proper summer sunshine with cold beers.

DAY 23

Luxury

With the extra weight of a sopping wet tent, a muddy groundsheet, and all the groceries kindly bought for me by Helen before she left, I felt a trepidation about setting off again.

Fortunately, all of my worries disappeared as soon as I started climbing the steep hill from Port Gaverne into Port Isaac.

I had already had an uplifting chat at the cove with two glorious early sea swimmers, before a fisherman stopped his car beside me.

He opened his driver's door and shouted out encouraging words, including telling me that after Port Quinn I was in for a 'luxury' walk.

The impressive set of steep granite steps leading out of Port Isaac made me excited to perhaps be about to transition from the slippery slate coast into grippy granite.

That was not yet to be the case, however, and I imagined that an excess of granite blocks may have been ordered when the harbour protection walls were built, with which it may have been decided to build this cliff staircase.

I'M NO SHAKESPEARE

I met several runners, on holiday but determinedly out for their usual exercise along the cliff path.

They all mentioned coffee in Port Quinn car park.

At Port Quinn, out of his converted horse box, Graham was setting up his business for the day, selling coffee, and the most wonderful rhubarb flapjack.

Graham was sixty two and had just been to the gym, and then straight afterwards had swam a mile.

He does this every day because in his words he is a 'grumpy fucker' in the mornings.

So he gets up early to work out, and to spare his family from the worst of his grumpiness.

I had obviously caught Graham in the sweet spot at the height of his gym and swimming endorphins, because he deliberately gave me a king sized Mars Bar for the price of a normal sized one.

I shared my Mars Bar with another hiker, who had been following me, and who had caught up with me at Graham's horse box.

Clive was younger than me and had all the gear.

He was interested in my kit and very knowledgeable.

He carried a sixty five litre backpack to my forty eight litre, which included five litres of water, plus purification tablets, plus a water filter.

He had however spent last night in a hotel in Port Isaac because of the rain, and had already had a full cooked breakfast.

I'M NO SHAKESPEARE

Clive's father, who was in his eighties, regularly sent his son clippings from the Times newspaper, in envelopes through the post.

Clive shared his father's latest dire warnings about cow attacks, and told me he would be finishing at Polzeath that day, as that was far enough for him.

I stopped for lunch overlooking Polzeath beach which was full of surfers and body boarders.

My left heel had been hurting for the past mile, so I removed my boots and socks to let my feet breathe and to inspect my sore area.

I hovered my penknife over my heel for some more fluid release surgery.

"What is that lady doing?

A dry-robed child asked its dry-robed parent.

"Is she cutting off her foot?"

"Er, no darling, I think she is just buttering a roll"

Was the clipped reply, as the child was ushered quickly past me.

At Daymer Bay, with no other option but to use the public toilets, I was shocked by the forty pence entrance fee, immediately followed by a curt recorded tannoy announcement warning that if you stayed too long the alarm would automatically activate.

Perhaps this is what the fisherman had meant by 'luxury'.

Jen and Rachel, two adventurous young women, had all day either been passing me or I had been passing them.

We met again, sharing the same ferry from Rock to Padstow.

I'M NO SHAKESPEARE

Once in bustling Padstow, full of crabbers, hair braiders, and the enticing aroma of fish and chips, I popped into Mountain Warehouse to purchase a spare gas cylinder and some water purification tablets.

My next priority was a cold beer and a good dinner, preferably next to an electric socket.

Richard, a young man serving in a small cafe just along from Mountain Warehouse, could not have been more welcoming.

Richard was a skateboarder from Wales who liked building his own decks.

He worked long shifts in the cafe and enjoyed wild camping and chatting.

He gifted me free croissants for the following morning's breakfast, and shared tips for some wild camping spots beyond Padstow, towards the beaches of Gun Point.

With my hunger fully satisfied by a steak and stilton pasty, my water bottles refilled, and my devices fully charged, I left Padstow to continue my evening search for a suitable camping spot.

DAY 24

Storm Antoni

Apart from having to spray insect repellent into my sleeping bag after somehow having carried biting ants into my netted sleeping pod, my night was calm and undisturbed.

At 0630, to the accompanying pastel colours of the early morning, I walked away from where I had pitched, at the edge of a cut straw field.

My tent was bone dry, and far lighter than yesterday.

Thirty minutes later I stopped on virgin yellow sands to wash my face in sea water, and to boil water for my porridge and coffee.

Richard's croissants had been a delicious midnight feast, as I had sat, cross-legged and snuggled into my down jacket.

I had been looking out of my porch towards flickering lights in the sand dunes of Rock, and wondering what secrets they held.

I saw only a very few early joggers and dog walkers on my walk towards Trevone.

I'M NO SHAKESPEARE

Then, on the edge of the cliffs, as Trevone with its busy bay and cafe came into view, I met Rupert, a fisherman, on holiday from Essex.

Rupert who had impressively ruddy cheeks, was carrying a huge rod, and had been trying for mackerel and then for bass, but with no luck.

He laughed that his family would be teasing him yet again over his lack of fishing prowess.

His humour and good nature were infectious, and we walked back down towards the bay together.

Then I peeled off, picking up speed, as I was lured to the cafe, a short walk away from the camper van filled carpark, by the aroma of a cooked breakfast.

I sensed a table of several people glancing across at my abysmal, street dog table manners as I devoured my Full Cornish breakfast.

I made a vain attempt to slow down, but my hunger was too fierce.

The day was set to be a comparatively easy one, a twenty three km section from bay to beautiful bay, via rocky island headlands.

This coast, with its barely submerged reefs, has always posed a significant risk to shipping.

The tide had been on its way out for most of the active beach going day, and every spare scrap of dry sand was claimed, territory marked with colourful beach umbrellas and windbreaks.

Families pulling carts, laden with supplies and small children, poured onto the beaches, and the lifeguards were busy with their

I'M NO SHAKESPEARE

binoculars, scanning the surfers and swimmers within their flagged areas, and keeping half an eye on those outside of them.

On the fine golden beach of Harlyn beach I stopped to recline for a while against a large warm slab of slate that was protruding at a perfect angle from the sand.

I boiled water and prepared hot chocolate, and enjoyed a rare feeling of warmth on my body, resting my head on the soft pillow of one of my stuff bags.

By the late afternoon the air had cooled and was starting to become damp.

The wind speed was increasing, and I was aware of yet another serious weather warning that had been issued for the following day.

Storm Antoni was on its way, with extreme strong gusts forecast, and the Met Office advice was to stay well away from all coastal areas.

On arriving at Porthcothan I made a safety based decision to catch the double decker Coaster bus back towards Newquay, and to stay at Watergate Bay Touring Park.

I have a huge German caravan of my own stored on this site so I know it well.

It has excellent laundry facilities, and a shop with a lively social bar area.

I was permitted to pitch my tent in the overnight arrivals area for half of the usual price of sixty four pounds for two nights.

It is a very expensive place, when my most expensive campsite to date has been just fifteen pounds per night.

I'M NO SHAKESPEARE

But it does boast an indoor swimming pool, a skate park, tennis courts, a large children's pirate ship play area, and is more holiday park than farmer's field.

Being Bingo night, the indoor bar and social area were crammed with large, loud groups and families, and it was a perverse relief to barely be able to hear my own thoughts.

I washed and dried my laundry in commercial machines, using a leading brand of non-bio powder, instead of my usual weak wristed hand wringing with any old hand soap, followed by an extended drip dry while swinging off my pack.

My tent was double pegged, tucked into a corner, with hedges on two sides, and hopefully would hold up in its usual admirable way to whatever Antoni decided to throw at it.

My plan was to catch the bus back to Porthcothan after the storm, and to resume from where I had stopped.

DAY 25

Waterproof Socks

The previous day I had passed by another beautifully inscribed bench.

I was not surprised to later learn that the words had been taken from another poem by Alfred, Lord Tennyson.

Break, Break, Break

    Break, break, break,

    On thy cold gray stones, O Sea!

    And I would that my tongue could utter

    The thoughts that arise in me.

    O, well for the fisherman's boy,

    That he shouts with his sister at play!

    O, well for the sailor lad,

    That he sings in his boat on the bay!

    And the stately ships go on

I'M NO SHAKESPEARE

To their haven under the hill;

But O for the touch of a vanish'd hand,

And the sound of a voice that is still!

Break, break, break

At the foot of thy crags, O Sea!

But the tender grace of a day that is dead

Will never come back to me.

So many benches are positioned looking out to sea in memory of loved ones, with their plaques commonly simply engraved, stating how much a much beloved family member or friend may have loved this place or view.

A whole life of an unknown person framed so publicly by the dates of their birth and their death.

Silhouetted strangers, resting on their benches, looking out to sea.

I often think, and especially when I am walking, of my little sister, Lynn, who was seven years younger than me.

As children, bouncing around in the back of a Ford Escort during the long journey from Devon to visit our grandparents in Surrey, my other sister and I would sing to her.

We sang her favourite songs, including this one, in harmonies that no doubt caused our mother to drive even faster to reach our destination.

Little donkey, little donkey

On the dusty road.

I'M NO SHAKESPEARE

Gotta keep on plodding onward

With your precious load.

The song was sung again, thirty nine years later, at Lynn's funeral.

I imagined what unwritten words I might read on her bench.

Rest here a while big sis.

Don't cry.

Come enter my sunbeam.

Pirouette with me, weightlessly,

And dance in silver dust, eternal.

So what did I do on yet another, weather stops play, enforced day off?

For starters, I bought a warm, sticky cinnamon swirl and a takeaway coffee for breakfast.

Rapidly followed by the embarrassment of getting myself locked in the men's toilet.

There had been two single toilets, side by side, both with clearly identifiable pictures of stick people.

One stick person with a flat bottomed triangle body, and the other with a pointy bottomed triangle body.

I had become confused and chosen a pointy bottom, but obviously did not possess the same sharpness of brain necessary to operate the lift and twist lock to get myself out.

I'M NO SHAKESPEARE

I banged loudly, and possibly quite madly, to attract the attention of a real man, before sauntering off nonchalantly, and perhaps slightly too brazenly over-egging my fly adjustment.

I caught the bus into Newquay, where the strength of the offshore gusts was forcing people to fight to stay upright on the pavements.

I treated myself to a pair of extortionately expensive waterproof socks called Sealskinz, an upgraded pair of Craghoppers waterproof trousers, and some more plasters.

I then found a cafe with a handy electric socket, where I drank coffee, watched people, and researched how to buy shares in Compeed.

The only thing more painful than a blister is having to replace a slipped, but perfectly reusable Compeed.

Not because of the physical pain, but because one Compeed is the monetary equivalent of a cinnamon swirl.

How can one fleshy plaster that looks and feels like dead heel-sloughed skin from the end of a Croc wearing Summer, that only has one solitary stick, and that leaves a solid gluey residue on my socks, to cause yet more blisters, be so expensive?

Back at the campsite the clubhouse was rocking.

I used to love it there, and it was not not so bad now either, sitting on a bar stool anonymously, warm, invisible, in my own world, with a charging point within reach.

The dinner that I had deliberately ordered, for its healthy spinach and salad, a lentil and chickpea dhal and a side salad, was delicious.

I'M NO SHAKESPEARE

A weak, early evening sunshine was highlighting the beer stains on my wooden table, and dogs lay under tables eating crumbs and dropped chips.

As a child, I had hated parties and discos and had always thought there was something wrong with me.

I know I disappointed my mother, who thought all teenagers must love discos and dancing.

I would always walk out, silently fighting back tears, feeling I had failed.

As I have matured there have definitely been parties that I have enjoyed, and even, very occasionally, usually after alcohol, I have danced.

Perhaps it would have been different if I had been exposed more to mad rhythm and movement as a tiny child, like the children here on the dance floor with their mums, dads, aunties, uncles, and grandparents.

If I had absorbed more of the craziness of adults letting go around me, teaching me how to express myself through illogical dance.

It is not that I am completely lacking in rhythm, or in social skills, rather that I am more of a private dancer than a John Travolta.

A dancer who, as much as she might secretly like to try, simply cannot bring herself to wiggle her body randomly in front of complete strangers.

DAY 26

Nafa

Storm Antoni had been short and sharp, and my tent had once again stood up well to its pummelling.

A dramatic sunset had appeared, and as the clouds began to clear, so the temperatures began to drop.

My personal hipometer certainly registered below ten degrees.

Then, just as the first warm morning rays of the sun started to increase the temperature inside my tent and to lull me finally into comfort, my alarm sounded.

The site cafe would not open until 0830, so I prepared my usual breakfast.

The bus that was due to arrive at 0820 failed to appear, and my smile and thumb only succeeded in attracting the attention of one kind lady, who was unfortunately not travelling in my direction.

I walked back to the cafe that was now open, and bought a cinnamon swirl and a second coffee, before returning to the bus stop to await the next scheduled Sunday bus.

I'M NO SHAKESPEARE

The bus stop was covered, full of books, and even boasted a moth eaten armchair with a comfortable cushion.

I started to read a heavy book called 'The Wolf Rider' by Katherine Russell, that I could not possibly have carried with me.

I considered the option of remaining in the luxury bus stop for a while longer.

At Mawgan Porth, however, I was due to rendezvous with my mother and her partner, so I needed to crack on.

The Cornish Coaster bus, with its optimistic open top deck, arrived punctually, and the driver replied to my cheery greeting with a grumpy warning:

"You, stay in your seat today! Not like yesterday!"

It was the same driver who yesterday afternoon had reprimanded me for standing and walking to the front of the bus before my stop.

Apparently I should have pressed the button and waited, as straight in my seat as Queen Victoria, and not moved until he had applied the handbrake.

I apologised, and assured him I would not move a single muscle.

At Porthcothan, with my feet back on the same sandy path that I had left two days ago, I skipped away from the bus, and towards my freedom.

A local fisherman joined me, heading out to the rocks to try for bass, and I passed holiday makers on their morning cliff top walks.

This section of path between Porthcothan and Mawgan Porth was busy in both directions, and I joined a stream of walkers traversing an open field of cows with their babies.

I'M NO SHAKESPEARE

The bovine mothers were on high alert, eyeballing everyone, and ready to organise themselves into trample formation at any sign of human or dog threat.

I kept my head down and quickened my pace.

The National Trust car park at Bedruthan was full, so I suppressed my craving for a pre-afternoon cream tea, and continued on towards Mawgan Porth.

There, on the path, just before I reached the busy beach of Mawgan Porth, was where I saw the approaching smiling faces of my mother and her partner.

After holding up the path traffic with lots of hugs, we all walked back together to Mawgan Porth and to the Merrymoor pub for lunch, where I caught up on family news and was let somewhat unwisely loose at a Carvery.

I have walked the section of path between Mawgan North and Newquay very many times, as it is the section where my caravan is sited.

I therefore made the decision to spend the afternoon with my family, and instead of walking, we looked down, from high above Lusty Glaze beach in Newquay, delighted but uninvited guests, to a private beach party, where beautiful and happy young people danced barefoot in the sand on their wedding day.

Shortly afterwards, at a brief stop at traffic lights in Newquay, to a hasty farewell, my pack, my poles, and I were bundled out of the car.

My bed that night, yes a real bed, was to be in a Backpacker's hotel in the centre of Newquay.

I'M NO SHAKESPEARE

The following day I would need to cross the Gannel estuary to continue walking towards Perranporth, and as this was an urban area with no camping sites, and too unsafe for street sleeping, I had opted for a night of pure luxury, with the sorcery of electricity and instant running hot water.

I had passed a barber's shop on my way to the hostel and had decided to pop my scruffy head around the door, and to enquire if anyone was up for the challenge.

Nafa, from Tunisia, had me aproned almost before I had removed my backpack.

Clutches of hair were grabbed and chunked, razors and clippers clicked and whirred, and I gulped at the amount of hair falling into my lap.

My head was roughly twisted from left to right, and my chin from up to down.

At the backpackers however, with my new haircut, I felt edgy and cool.

That feeling very quickly disappeared when the receptionist told me that she would generate an 'easy' door code for me, because:

"People usually use an App."

She did stop short of actually explaining to me what an App was, but the damage was already done.

It was not a bad room in which to lick the wounds of a bruised ego, with A picture window, above the head of a soft white duveted double bed, with a view directly down onto the low tide expanse of Towan Beach.

I'M NO SHAKESPEARE

The room contained a kettle with tea bags and milk, my own private shower room, and a TV that may possibly have been bigger than the bed.

I may actually have forgotten what a TV is, and perhaps I should have gone back downstairs to the receptionist to ask her to explain.

After drinking two beakers of tea, I hung my ground sheet up to dry in my room and ventured downstairs to the backpacker's bar.

It was heaving with Australian bar staff, nubile young surfers, and underage security officers, and a solo guitarist was singing his heart out.

The tide was almost fully in, and I found a seat by a window where I could enjoy the atmosphere and the music, and watch the messy, footprint covered last patches of sand being once more washed clean.

Twice a day, since forever, the Atlantic has pushed right up to the base of the cliffs, to cleanse and smooth the sands.

Jacob was from London and had just arrived in Newquay by train.

From the following day he would be working as a security guard at the huge Boardmasters music festival that was in the process of being set up above Watergate Bay.

The following weekend would see an influx of festival goers and campers to the area.

I hoped to have put some more miles between myself and Newquay by the start of the festival, but I was interested to hear about Jacob's life and his work.

I'M NO SHAKESPEARE

As a child he had wanted to be a mechanic, but had fallen into IT and concept solutions, and in his spare time he liked to travel to go snowboarding in Japan.

After sharing a beer and very pleasant conversation, I bade him a polite goodnight and hurried back upstairs to bounce, I mean rest, on my massive mattress.

DAY 27

Adder

How very strange it was to have proper pillows, and to go to bed without wearing three layers of clothing and thick socks, and without my down jacket hood pulled snugly around my ears.

Adjacent to my room was a steep stair well and a heavy fire door, and I was disturbed, until the early hours, by the sounds of other residents, returning to the busy mixed sex dorms on this second floor.

At 0700 I was woken by the cries of the harbour seagulls.

The sun was already bright, and the tide, which had crept fully out again during the night, was on its inexorable way back in.

High tide would be reached at 1000 and, for an hour or so either side of this, the Gannel estuary would be able to be crossed by small ferry.

My plan, after tea and an attempt to calm my newly razored hair, was to walk from the hostel to the Fern Pit cafe, from where the ferry would hopefully carry me safely across to Crantock Beach.

I'M NO SHAKESPEARE

If, for any reason, the ferry were not operating, I would face a long detour inland.

Newquay in the early morning sunshine was quite surprisingly attractive, and did not resemble the town I have only known during bustling Summer opening hours or stag and hen partied evenings.

Laid back breakfasters and coffee drinkers, some who had already been for a dawn swim, were sitting, relaxed, at outdoor cafe tables.

Construction workers were already sweating on the many half built multi-storey blocks, while people in uniforms and wearing identification lanyards walked past purposefully to their work in shops, offices, cafes, and care homes.

I arrived at the Fern Pit cafe half an hour before the gate to its attractive tea garden was unlocked.

Resting a while beside a wooden picnic table, I enjoyed the panoramic view down and across the estuary towards Crantock beach.

In contrast to the standup paddle boarders who were lazily traversing the tranquil waters of the Gannel, there was a complete frenzy taking place on Crantock beach.

There, like Wild West settlers with their wagons, the folding beach trolley haulers, were staking their claims to prime sand.

The ferryman was waiting for me at the foot of the steep steps that wound from the cafe down through a beautiful tropical garden of ferns and brightly coloured flowers.

He reached out a warm and steady hand, offering support as I stepped into his small wooden boat.

I'M NO SHAKESPEARE

My sense of touch was heightened after so long without such human contact.

After exploring the maze of narrow paths that wound through the spiked grass and dunes at Crantock, I found my way back to the coast path.

I had not eaten since the excesses of yesterday's carvery, and was beginning to feel the unwanted effects of an unplanned intermittent fast.

After a mile of walking I was therefore easily lured, a few steps away from the path, to a modern hotel and spa complex with chrome and glass balconies and tennis courts.

I chose a table downwind of the beautifully dressed clientele, whose children were delicately drinking lemon tea, and I ordered a coffee, and the most incredible full English, that I later judged to be the best breakfast of the entire path.

A few miles after breakfast I very nearly leapt, Scooby Doo style, into the arms of a handsome wetsuited man.

Simon had been swimming with seals, but had popped up to the headland with his mobile phone to try to get a signal for some work he had to deal with.

I walked past him as he stood in concentration, looking at his phone.

"I've just seen a snake!" he exclaimed.

I yelped, jumped, and did some further ridiculous instinctive walking over hot coals leg movements.

I am sure Tarzan would not have been so pathetic around serpents.

I'M NO SHAKESPEARE

"Look!"

Simon grinned, and shoved his phone screen under my nose like a naughty little brother.

"I videoed it!"

The video, of the biggest snake I had ever seen, invoked a primaeval shudder, and for the rest of the day I was on high alert, adder watch, barely looking at the sea.

I only truly relaxed when I crossed the three mile expanse of Perran sands, walking as close to the sea as possible, where I was almost certain that snakes would never venture.

I really do not mind spiders, and I often pick them up and move them to safety if they stray into my tent.

Snakes though, are quite another matter.

It had occurred to me that Simon might have made a lovely son in law, so, not quite as daft as I must have appeared, I managed to secure his phone number by asking him to WhatsApp me his video.

I arrived at Perranporth at just after 1500, still feeling strong, and undecided about whether to stop there as I had planned, or to continue towards St. Agnes.

After a rest and a pint in the very comfortable Seiner's Arms, my telephone was charged and my mind was made up, to continue onwards.

The weather was still calm and dry, but rain was again forecast for the following day, so I chose to walk on, unencumbered by waterproofs.

From the cliffs beyond Perranporth I entered the very different landscapes of the old mining coast.

I'M NO SHAKESPEARE

From the pub, I had called ahead to a small campsite called Blue Hills, where a backpacker's pitch was being saved for me.

Blue Hills was situated very close to the path, before St. Agnes, and had the best facilities and hottest showers of any site I have visited.

My pitch did have a gentle slope, which I overcame by wedging my crocs under my mattress, as very effective anti slip devices.

It felt good to be snuggled up again in my tent.

DAY 28

Bottom Shaft

On another wet morning, with the smell of damp grass and earth both surrounding me and a part of me, I stood at the sink in the campsite washroom and cupped my hands to splash water against my face.

My hair dries naturally each night, stuffed into a tight buff and covered by the hood of my down jacket, and I smiled at my wild reflection.

I looked tanned and relaxed, especially in the soft focus without my glasses.

Beside me stood a friendly camper, wearing uggs and a onesie and carefully applying her cleansing products, moisturiser, and make-up.

She freed her damp hair from a towel twist, and reached for the hairdryer.

Our respective basic needs for water, hygiene, and kind social contact were satisfied, and our similarities were far greater than our differences.

I'M NO SHAKESPEARE

Hopping back over the wall from the campsite, to return to the coast path, I immediately came across Steve and Larissa, early bird walkers, with big smiles and rosy cheeks.

They explained how they had been following the Celtic Way, a new pilgrimage route covering one hundred and twenty five miles through Cornwall from St. German's to St. Michael's Mount.

The route incorporates over sixty miles of the Cornish coastal path, as well as two established pilgrimage routes: The Saints' Way and St. Michael's Way.

The website states that the Celtic Way is divided into sixteen walks that can be done as a whole over about two weeks or can be completed in sections over a longer period of time.

Steve and Larissa had hired a luggage transport company to take care of the daily transport of their sleeping bags and mattresses to various church halls, where accommodation is provided for a low cost to those who hold the trail Passport.

From St. Agnes, where I stopped in a beach cafe for a coffee and a Snickers bar, the predominant landscape was a purple and yellow carpet of low heather and gorse, with contrasting dark brooding granite towers and mineshaft heads.

For safety, many mines have been capped with rusty, conical, metal lattices, and I childishly failed to keep a straight face on passing a solemn looking plaque that informs visitors that in May 1998 Wheal Sally's Bottom Shaft was plugged by Kerrier District Council.

This area is now visited by walkers and holidaying families, but not so long ago it was the blood and sweat home to hard working

I'M NO SHAKESPEARE

Cornishmen and women, the air filled with their shouts, the sound of machinery, and human effort.

Many men made their fortunes from tin mining, and many died.

At Porthtowan, with still no sign of the forecasted dry weather, I stopped for a lunch of fish and chips, and a pint, in the Unicorn pub.

Feeling particularly sleepy after my lunch, it was a slow wander onwards to Portreath, stopping too to chat to two young German hikers, Lisa and Steffi, who were overtaking me.

They had found an inland campsite for the evening, so were hurrying to reach Portreath in time to catch a bus.

My plan was to carry on past Portreath to search for a wild camping spot, and what a location I found.

As I was congratulating myself on having found such a perfect grassed clifftop square looking towards the sunset and the slowly clearing clouds, Dimitry, a very charming young Ukrainian, stopped to offer help.

I am quite adept now at setting up my camp single handedly, but you know what I am like.

After a good chat with Dimitry, my new Facebook friend, a goodbye, and a big thank you, I made hot tea with an individually wrapped bag saved from the Newquay Backpacker's hostel, and I snuggled once more into my warm bag.

DAY 29

Penelope

As forecasted, the wind abated during the night.

I slept well and began packing away my camp at 0715.

Each morning it takes an hour of steady, slow, warming, activity to repack and to be ready to set off again.

On unzipping my tent, only a foot of grass was visible before the face of a thick, white, claggy mist.

As there was no wind, the mist was in no hurry to lift.

Doubly hungry this morning, and invisible, in the mist, to any early path walkers, I prepared twice my usual quantity of porridge.

Spider webs hung wetly on brambles in the quiet misty air, and I picked especially delicious blackberries on my way towards Hayle.

In a layby, after a mile, I was greeted by Arthur, a friendly and open young man wearing leopard print fleece trousers and living full time out of his converted van.

Arthur was a musician and a songwriter who, after breakfast, was heading to Falmouth to record music with a friend.

I'M NO SHAKESPEARE

His van was a colourful mixture of hand built wood panelling, with exotic animal print wall and door coverings.

At Godrevy head, after stopping to observe a protected colony of seals on a beach, I met Caroline who was a local and my age.

Caroline used to be a postlady and still loved walking, having recently completed the Dartmoor perambulation, and soon to be travelling to the Mendips to explore the hills there.

She told me where to buy the best pasties in St. Ives, and warned me to be especially vigilant for adders when crossing the Hayle sand dunes.

I blanched visibly and considered catching a bus.

As I approached a National Trust cafe at Godrevy I caught up with Charles, my age, who was wearing a fluorescent National Trust logoed jacket and picking up litter with metal prongs.

I was curious about his life and job, and we walked and chatted for a while together as he worked.

As well as litter picking, Charles deals with maintaining the cleanliness, restocking, and good functioning of the toilets and the car park machines and his job is varied and responsible.

He described the best part of his job as seeing the resurgence of birds and nature, and described to me how the National Trust have spent 30,000 pounds in an initiative to rewild three fields, between Hartland and Bude, and will continue to re-seed from these areas.

Charles walks an average of twelve kms per day, covering several areas in Cornwall, and on his lunch breaks and in his spare time he surfs.

I'M NO SHAKESPEARE

He started surfing as a young teenager at Bantham beach close to his hometown of Kingsbridge, where I was also based, for twenty years at the town's ambulance station, and we had lots to chat about.

Charles continued litter picking, and I stopped at the National Trust cafe for a Breakfast Special of a sausage, bacon and egg filled ciabatta, and a sweet coffee.

The tide was fully out, so I opted to minimise the risk of seeing any of Caroline's adders, by walking along the huge expanse of Hayle beach.

I stripped for a welcome morning bathe, scrubbing myself and my clothes with the fine sand and letting the waves tumble us clean.

Walking slowly onwards across the sand to the river estuary, I stepped carefully over piles of razor shells and pulled apart body bits of crabs.

I filled my water bottles at an outdoor beer garden, and downed a cool beer, before heading inland for a long walk around the Hayle Estuary.

I passed a poignant memorial to Rick Rescorla.

Originally from Hayle, Rick had died, with many of his fire service colleagues, in the 2001 Twin Tower Terrorist attack in New York.

As an eighteen year old, I had walked between the two towers, and I clearly remembered the strength of the wind being funnelled around the bases of the two great structures.

Further towards the crossing at the head of the estuary I rested in the cafe of a large Asda store, at a quiet table next to a charging socket.

I'M NO SHAKESPEARE

For the next few days I would be passing around the remote far South West peninsula, where opportunities for refreshments would be limited.

I therefore decided to buy a few more sachets of hot chocolate, some dried noodles, a small tin of baked beans, and more flapjack and chocolate.

Provisions to see me safely through to Penzance if necessary.

It was always reassuring to know that I was carrying a good amount of food and water, but the weight of these extra supplies was certainly felt.

Even one or two kilograms above my base weight adds a significant extra strain to my amazing feet.

My plan had been to carry on past the town of St. Ives for a second night of wild camping, but time was getting on, so this was open to change.

Navigating the Hayle estuary was a very long trudge, during which I lost time by taking a wrong turn, and became tired and grumpy.

As I was walking to St Ives, I picked fresh lavender for some calming aromatherapy, rubbed it stealthily under my armpits, and chatted with countless dog walkers.

The coast path cut through the cocktail gardens of some exclusive hotels in Carbis Bay, where there was a stark juxtaposition between the salty skinned hiker, bowed forwards under the weight of her pack, hobbling due to already having covered almost twenty three kms, and the prim, perfumed, and elegantly coiffured clientele reclining on Tattinger logoed outdoor furniture in manicured gardens.

I'M NO SHAKESPEARE

It was already 1900 when I arrived into the thronged streets of St. Ives, and to carry on to the far coast, away from the evening walkers and joggers, would have taken too much time.

So I decided to move to Plan B, and to investigate whether there were any available hostel beds in the town.

Fate again on my side, I was able to book the last bed in the Cohort Hostel in the centre of St. Ives, where I was allocated a high top bunk in an eight bedded mixed dormitory.

I hauled my backpack up to my bed, and planned to leave early the next morning to continue walking towards the tiny granite village of Zennor.

I initially lay on my bed feeling exhausted and ready to fall asleep, but a gnawing hunger led me to take my packet of mashed potatoes, tin of beans and two Baby Bels downstairs to the communal kitchen.

It was there that I met Penelope, who was seventy one, and who had been living in the hostel for seven weeks.

Penelope was from Peterborough, where she lived with her husband who was a barrister.

In June they had both been in Bude attending their daughter's two day wedding celebrations.

After the wedding the newlyweds headed off to Glastonbury, but refused to allow Penelope to accompany them.

Penelope's children and husband told her she was too old to go to a festival, so Penelope, in a fit of pique, caught the train to the far West of Cornwall, where she stayed in hostels and occasionally with strangers.

I'M NO SHAKESPEARE

She had bought herself a wetsuit and a dry robe and was cooking herself fresh mussels and salad in the hostel kitchen before going out, in her words, "on the town".

Penelope's favourite pastime was to browse the beaches and galleries, to buy expensive artwork and to have it couriered back to her husband, and she had been learning to surf.

Being Catholic and having been educated in a strict convent school, Penelope had also been attending Mass in St. Ives, wearing just her dressing gown under her dry robe.

Her hair was styled in a very beautiful white-blonde long bob, and on starting to chat, as I was mixing my beans into my instant mashed potatoes, she kindly offered me a glass of Pimms.

Penelope's husband would dearly like her to return home, but she was having none of it, and did not want to go home to, in her words "wash socks and sit on the sofa".

Her husband had tried to buy her a ticket on a sleeper train, which she had cancelled, and she had deliberately lost the power bank he had given her, so that he could not interrupt her fun or demand that she speak to him.

She was a complete loon, and although I was not immune to the bemused sideways glances from the other residents, who had no doubt learned to keep a polite distance, we got on like a house on fire.

DAY 30

Zennor

I had definitely hit the jackpot dorm, the one with no resident snorers, and on my high mattress platform, under a freshly laundered white duvet, with my privacy curtain tightly closed, I slept deeply.

Penelope and I met again on the stairs at 0800, as I was leaving the hostel to start my walk around the end of the world.

She was getting ready to attend a private drawing class, ever curious and eager for more adventures.

The walk to Zennor village took only four hours, including a stop at an Neolithic cist where I absorbed some of the magic of West Penwith, and made hot chocolate to accompany my cinnamon and apple breakfast bars.

It was a section as hard as any in North Devon, requiring me to clamber over huge granite boulders, to balance on thick tufts of grass, to hop over boggy areas, and to follow muddy streams steeply uphill.

I'M NO SHAKESPEARE

As I detoured inland from the path, to approach the village of Zennor, a thick, wet mist descended.

The views of the sea became obscured, and I started to feel chilled.

Two hours in the old granite Tinners Arms with some local beer, and a huge plate of home reared ham, hot chips, and locally produced eggs, slowly dried and warmed me.

According to the landlady there was a summer pop-up camping field less than a mile away, which was exactly where I went.

I intended to take my time and to enjoy every step of this severe and remote section of the path, in this mystical land of hurled granite and turquoise sea.

DAY 31

Pendeen

The Tinners Arms was built in 1271.

Tinners Ale is the local's favourite beer, and it is strong stuff.

Two pints sipped slowly over lunch, led to a good twelve hours of sleep, but I suppose a little tiredness was to be expected as, according to the South West Coast Path distance calculator, I had now been walking for over two hundred and forty miles.

There was no shower in my camping field, just a wonky portaloo, and in the early evening a very handsome farmer, with a gorgeous Cornish accent, drove his clean, black Land Rover Discovery around the field.

He greeted new campers with a portable card reader and kindly handed out bottles of fresh drinking water.

In the morning, to refill my water bottles, it was necessary to call in to the farmhouse, to use its outdoor tap.

You would have thought that after so much sleep, and in full view of the said farmer, I might have been awake enough not to try to attach a hosepipe to an electric car charging socket.

I'M NO SHAKESPEARE

Walking back through Zennor and past the Tinners Arms towards the coast path, I spotted a large flat slab of granite with a hollowed basin in its centre, with a plaque that read:

'Zennor Plague Stone' was positioned here at the boundary of Zennor Churchtown during outbreaks of disease. The depression in the centre was filled with vinegar. Money that changed hands between villagers and outsiders would be placed in the vinegar and thus disinfected.

The main cholera epidemics in Cornwall struck during the years 1832 and 1849.

Zennor to Pendeen took another five hours of hard hiking, including a lunch stop to cook salty chicken noodles and sweet hot chocolate.

I saw no other human, but did bravely spot my first adder that was crossing the path directly in front of me, as I was being guided by dragonflies and butterflies.

Intuitive guardians, butterflies appear before me always when I most need them.

The whoosh of colour between every wing beat encourages me, and I thank them and send love, before they flit softly from my vision.

I camped at Pendeen in another basic field, but this time with a portable shower that I bravely tested.

Running into cold waves without wearing a wetsuit can be exhilarating.

Standing naked in a wooden, open topped and open bottomed cubicle, like an extra in a Carry On film, waiting for the non-existent hot water to appear, while everyone on the site could see every

I'M NO SHAKESPEARE

frantic avoidant foot movement and could hear every blasphemous word, and no doubt witness that I was simultaneously urinating with the shock of the continuous stream of ice cold spring water from the malevolent spraying tap, was not quite so exhilarating.

There was barely any protection from the strengthening winds, blowing strongly now from the Atlantic, and I was concerned about how my tent, cord, and pegs would cope with the gusts.

As a precaution, I again stored all my belongings inside my sleeping pod, and with no nearby Ale House, ancient or modern, I drank miserable black tea with my rehydrated dehydrated dinner.

I comforted myself with the thought that the following day I would be entering historic mining museum country, aka the deliciousness of National Trust cafes.

DAY 32

Copper Kettle

According to the Met office, overnight wind of just thirty three kilometres per hour had been gusting at Pendeen.

My tent had definitely previously stood up to similar wind strength, but these gusts were short sharp tugs that sounded like gunshots, and that tested every stitch of my tent and of the peg cords.

One cord did snap, the one that I had noticed was already slightly frayed from the evening of wild camping on the cliffs with Helen, where I had used heavy, sharp slate as extra anchoring weight.

In this compact earth all the pegs had held well, but a lesson had been learned.

I decided to take time to add extra loops of paracord to each tarp fixing, to be ready for use instantly in case of future failures.

Despite having been the Patrol Leader of the Scarlet Pimpernel Brownie Six, I could still only tie granny knots: right over left and under, left over right and under.

I hoped they would be strong enough.

I'M NO SHAKESPEARE

Due to the wind, breakfast was again prepared inside my tent, with my ground sheet and pack pulled well away from any danger of a fallen stove.

At 0800 I stood raggedly on the clifftops, as the strong salty wind blasted me fully awake.

Information boards at Levant mine told the story of copper and arsenic mining, with a respectful memorial to the miners who lost their lives in one of Cornwall's worst mining disasters.

On the afternoon of October 20th, 1919, the linkage between the engine and rod in the Man-engine Shaft broke and thirty one men plunged to the deepest levels of the mine, to their deaths.

A horizontal rain shower slammed into me as I walked towards Cape Cornwall, making it necessary to pull on my new waterproof trousers.

Then, as I approached the valley before the beautiful Cape, the clouds cleared and she was bathed in morning sunshine, all the clearer after the rain.

At the Cape I met Tina, a local for generations, from a family of butchers.

Tina was walking her two dogs and we stopped to discuss the exorbitant cost of seven hundred pounds for adder antivenom from the veterinary surgery.

Tina carried antihistamines in her pocket just in case her dogs were to be bitten.

She also told me that in cities no one is ever more than a few feet away from a rat, but that out here on this coast you could substitute rat for adder.

I'M NO SHAKESPEARE

I turned pale and quickly inland towards the small town of St. Just where I took a table at a small cafe called the 'Copper Kettle'.

Tina's family supplies the 'Copper Kettle' with meat, and she had recommended it to me as the best place for a Full Cornish breakfast.

She told me that I must tell them that Tina had sent me.

Down here in Kernow, if you want to make friends and influence people, you must never, ever refer to a Full Cornish as a Full English.

In the 'Copper Kettle' I met Jackie, who cooked me an incredible feast including hogs and black puddings.

In case she had not already guessed, I mentioned my pressing need for a launderette, and Jackie recommended Steve at the Sea View campsite in Sennen, who she said was very nice and had a washing machine.

And she told me that I must tell him that Jackie had sent me.

After stocking up with more of my favourite chocolate, and instant mashed potato, of which I had just discovered the holy grail of a cheesy version, I began navigating over fields to find my way back to the coast path.

Ancient granite stiles always delighted me, wondering who had laid them and whose feet had previously climbed them.

I met Rudolph, as I rejoined the path, a German who, with his wife, had been working on a vegetable farm for two weeks, harvesting and weeding.

I'M NO SHAKESPEARE

They were both now taking some time for themselves, and planned to walk the path from St Just and around the far west peninsula of Land's End.

As I approached the luminous white sands of Whitesand Bay, at Sennen Cove, I recalled the many previous times I had been here.

In my early twenties, it had been one of my favourite places, and still held secret memories.

Over thirty years later only the beach, car park, and lifeboat station matched my memories.

The lovely old pub, The 'Old Success', had been given an ugly modern extension of holiday lets, and was closed for a private function.

So, Instead of a pint there, for memory sake, I bought an ice cream and watched as strong waves pushed young laughing boys in wetsuits from the harbour wall.

Most of the dwelling houses in the cove are now holiday lets, and many new exclusive houses have been built higher up overlooking the bay.

I walked slowly away and inland to make my way across more fields towards the Sea View camping park.

Thirty five years ago it had been no more than a large camping field, with a small reception, and my little children had played there on its single swing.

Now it is a large corporate site, with a swimming pool, and adventure playground, and is filled with static caravans.

Steve was enjoying a day off, but Holly was a true campsite angel and could not have been more lovely.

I'M NO SHAKESPEARE

My clothes were washed and dried, I showered in the most amazing hot water, and my pitch was level and sheltered on three sides.

The iconic 'First and Last Inn', a short walk away from where I was staying, was also nothing as I recalled.

The building's granite facade was familiar, but the inside, full of large groups of holidaying families, had been modernised.

I chose a nostalgic pint of Jail Ale, a Dartmoor beer from my home area.

DAY 33

Lands' End

On leaving the toilet in the First and Last Inn, I was thrilled to be reminded, by a glassed over deep granite tunnel and an information wall poster, of a certain horrible history of this public house which reads as follows:

Circa 1620

The entrance to Smugglers Tunnel, running to the cliffs.

'Annie's Well'

Former landlady Ann Treeve presided over smuggling and wrecking operations together with the local parson, before turning Queen's evidence against Dionysius, a Sennen farmer (the smuggling agent) who then served a long prison sentence. For Annie's 'service' to the crown she was staked out on Sennen beach and drowned by the incoming tide. Her body was laid out in the large upstairs room in this inn prior to the burial in an unmarked grave, for fear of retribution by way of grave robbers.'

Please don't step on the glass.

I'M NO SHAKESPEARE

The Inn's website additionally informs that Anne still has her room at the inn, and to this day people who stay there have reported having dreams of drowning and seeing the figure of a lady lurking on the landing.

I walked back through fine drizzling rain to my tent, insatiably curious to follow that smuggler's tunnel out to the cliffs.

When I was a child I loved playing Cowboys and Indians and had colourful plastic figures and a tiny teepee with a bonfire around which I would place my Red Indian figures.

I had always wanted a wigwam of my own, attempting to fashion wobbly ones out of sticks and sheets.

That morning, as I sat cross legged and watched the sunrise from my pyramid, cradling my Horlicks like Hiawatha, my excitement and my urge to whoop and dance around my stove, was barely contained.

I was about to round Land's End, to change direction, the setting sun to be at my back, and to swap the Atlantic Ocean for the English Channel.

At the gates of the huge Land's End complex of shops, hotels, cafes and various visitor exhibitions, a group of lycra clad cyclists were preparing to head off to John O'Groats.

The only coffee to be found that early was in the large hotel, so I continued walking, and stopped to made my own coffee beside the quiet cliff tops, looking out towards the Longships lighthouse.

Waves were crashing around the rocks on which the lighthouse stands, and from whose peril it protects all those at sea.

Much further out in the roughest waves, several large container ships were entering and leaving the English Channel, which is the

I'M NO SHAKESPEARE

busiest shipping lane in the world, with over four hundred vessel transits every day.

At a refreshment hut and garden approaching Porthgwarra, I was greeted once again by Rudolph, and by his wife Una, who waved, smiled, and kindly treated me to coffee.

We sat together at a picnic bench where I learned that Rudolph was an actor by profession.

He had had his own business for many years, travelling all over Germany and storytelling to children and adults of all ages in schools and libraries.

At Porthcurno, due to the amount of visitors, even a simple viewing entry to the Minack theatre, a stone, clifftop, open air theatre, was reserved for pre-booked ticket holders only.

I had visited several times before, including to watch a Shakespeare play to the awe inspiring backdrop of the sea.

For Rudolph and Una it was particularly disappointing not to be able to enter to witness the granite hewn stage and seating.

We parted at the beach as it was beginning to rain and they had both decided to catch a bus back to Sennen.

I continued to climb up out of the bay towards Treen, where I found a comfortable small campsite just off the path.

It was raining heavily and was forecast to continue all evening.

The air was damp and cold, and my intention, if the warm comfort of the Logan Rock Inn did not tempt me to walk the mile down the lane to the village, was to snuggle up early after a hot dinner of corned beef and cheesy mashed potatoes.

DAY 34

Markus

As the central heating effect of the hot mashed potato began to fade, I once more started to feel cold from the toes upwards.

My new Sealskinz waterproof socks came to the rescue, and redeemed themselves for their extortionate cost.

I pulled them over my thin merino bed socks, and what a game changer they were.

I'm no gran who wrote a porno, but the warmth generated by those socks rose from my toes through my whole body in a wave of pure pleasure and relief.

After waiting for the early rain to pass, and for the promising band of clear sky to approach the coast from France, I set off towards Penzance.

The route was quiet, muddy in places, and included a traverse of a bouldered beach.

There were also some steep and overgrown areas where I used my poles to push the brambles away from my face.

I'M NO SHAKESPEARE

As I approached Lamorna I met several day walkers including a young boy from Tipperary who told me he was afraid of ducks.

I was also overtaken by Markus from Germany, another walker who had started from Minehead.

We stopped to chat, before I dived into the Lamorna cafe to buy a large steak pasty.

"I do not eat until the afternoon" said Markus, and he hurried on.

I thought of my porridge and the two Twix's I had already consumed, and I wondered if I may have picked up some parasites from all my mucky living and sleeping on grass.

Then Chris, another through-hiker, greeted me, entered the cafe, and emerged with a large steak pasty AND chips.

We both talked a lot about food and how hungry we got, and how we would fight each other for the last cheesy instant mashed potato on a supermarket shelf.

Chris knew his stuff as he had also previously walked from Lands' End to John O Groats.

I was therefore reassured that hiker's constant hunger was perfectly normal and non parasitic, and that Markus' non hunger must just be a German thing.

I left Chris and his dog at the café and continued towards Mousehole, passing the clifftop memorial to the crew of the Solomon Browne lifeboat and to the crew and passengers of the Union Star.

Sixteen lives, all lost in the Penlee lifeboat disaster in December 1981.

I'M NO SHAKESPEARE

Mousehole village was busy with August holidaymakers and was where I executed my second dive.

Into the open door of a very welcoming pub above the harbour.

I was just finishing my beer when Chris walked in and over to me.

"Hello!" I said, "You had the same idea then?!"

"Of course I did, it's a pub!" he replied, laughing.

To be kind to his dog's paws, Chris was planning to catch a bus through the next urban section, Newlyn to Penzance.

I left to carry on walking along the seafront, and I eventually arrived at another Summer pop-up campsite, Ponsandane, on the far edge of Penzance.

It was a perfect location from where to continue towards the Lizard peninsula, which was now visible.

From my tent entrance, whilst finishing my dinner, I saw Markus.

Quite possibly in a confused state of hypoglycaemia, he was wandering on the inland side of the railway line.

He was close to my campsite and appeared to be trying to find his way back to the path, to the beach side of the railway tracks.

I would have offered to cook him a good meal of baked beans stirred into cheesy mash, but I had just finger-licked the last of it from my pot.

I was camped next to another German, a lone motorcyclist, the strong silent type, who had proceeded to hang his pheromone

I'M NO SHAKESPEARE

ridden leather biking trousers like a Bundesflagge from the large tree under which we were both camped.

I watched covertly as he competently cooked several healthy looking ingredients, separately.

Then he sat at our communal wooden picnic table to dine, with a glass of wine.

Probably appalled by my heathen slop, non-existent table manners, and my socks that I had hung, perhaps a little impolitely, too close to his trousers, he totally ignored me.

For a pop-up campsite Ponsandane had the best showers yet, surpassing even the Caravan Club luxury shower block at Boscastle.

There were spacious, private rooms containing a walk in shower with scalding hot water, toilet and sink.

DAY 35

Slate Heart

I slept wonderfully after a hot shower, and at 0830 I set off along the concrete boardwalk towards Marazion.

St. Michael's Mount was already attracting visitors, silhouetted like ants in the low morning sunshine, as they traversed the low tide causeway.

Somewhere along the north Cornwall slate coast I had stopped to pick up a perfect heart shaped piece of slate, no larger than the palm of my hand.

I had been carrying it with me ever since, not wanting to part with it, but knowing that carrying emotional nonsense, that is not in any way practically useful, just adds unnecessary weight.

A cottage in Marazion caught my eye.

On its one downstairs windowsill were sitting a collection of different sized and shaped slate hearts.

I opened the gate, walked a few steps past the small wild flower filled patch of front garden, and rang the bell.

I'M NO SHAKESPEARE

The owner's suspicion turned to delight as I introduced my heart, and asked if they would please adopt it to place with all their other hearts.

A little way beyond Marazion I met Irene, from Bideford.

Irene was seventy five years old, and she was walking from Perranuthnoe to Mousehole.

Before her husband's death, six years ago, they had both set themselves a challenge to complete the South West Coast Path together, a section at a time.

Irene had been intent on continuing to walk on, alone, in his memory.

Her grandson was now seventeen and accompanied her to lend a steady arm on the tricker sections.

I soon reached Perranuthnoe where, as Irene had promised, a superb beach cafe with an equally superb all day breakfast bap awaited me.

From Perranuthroe onwards the terrain became much tougher, with descents into many beautiful sandy coves, followed by steep climbs with no rest before the next descent.

I walked for a short while with Linda, now from London, but originally from Appledore.

She told me stories of a happy childhood spent on the remote beaches around Hartland Point.

Linda was enjoying a few days walking sections of the path around the Lizard, sea swimming from the rocks wherever possible.

Walking in hot sunshine was extra thirsty work that required a second refreshment stop.

I'M NO SHAKESPEARE

At Praa Sands my water bottles were refilled, a kindness that I always appreciate, and I sat with a cold beer at a café terrace overlooking the beach.

I watched the many body boarders shrieking as they caught the perfect, close to shore, breaking waves.

On leaving Praa sands I met Andrew from Surrey.

Andrew was in Cornwall for a few days of solo walking, staying in bed and breakfast accommodation.

He was required back in Surrey for golf commitments, and was on a mission to cover as many miles as quickly as possible.

He sped off, like most people do, at more than double my shuffling pace.

As the afternoon wore on, and the sun dropped lower, the sea began to shimmer.

I passed the ruins of more mine buildings, starkly contrasted against the silver sea.

Tom had been out all day with his clients, climbing on the cliffs.

He was carrying rope and climbing equipment, and still had a long walk home to Praa Sands.

He was a cheerful young man, and he stopped to share his experiences of coast path walking and camping.

After twenty three km I reached a campsite in Porthleven, attached to the historic 'Out Of The Blue' freehouse, which is also home to the Porthleven Museum that showcases the town's history.

The showers there were once again set to many wonderful degrees above tepid, the young barman, Fraser, was naturally kind

I'M NO SHAKESPEARE

and welcoming, and a pint of the locally brewed Spingo Ale went down extremely well.

DAY 36

Lizard

The next morning, with no wind and a colder than usual overnight temperature, the dew was heavy.

While I ate my porridge, I hung my groundsheet and tent over a wooden fence, facing the rising sun.

By 0800 it was already hot, and it took just ten minutes for them to fully dry.

Leaving Porthleven I was saved by a pastor.

Glen was sitting in his black car at the far end of an empty car park.

The coast path is usually very well signposted by the sign of an acorn.

In this car park, unusually, there was no acorn, but two visible paths.

I was heading, obviously, for the more dangerous and exciting looking path, at the far end of the car park.

I'M NO SHAKESPEARE

Not yet realising that this path, once chosen, would then drop straight off the cliff.

Glen, Project Development Manager at Harvesters Ministries, wound down his window, warned me, and pointed towards the second, more righteous, path.

Glen was fascinating to chat with.

It turned out that he was not lurking with questionable intent, but praying.

He had travelled all over the world with his church work and I asked many questions, which he was kind enough to answer.

He gave me his card and I researched the Harvesters Ministries website.

"How do you plant more than 70 new churches every day? We use a unique strategy called 'Saturation Mapping' to multiply new communities of born-again believers.

Harvesters Ministries is Opening the Way by training pastors to know the Word, disciple believers, evangelise the lost and plant churches in every community around the world.

Our vision is to plant 1 million churches, to train 1 million pastors, and evangelise and disciple 100 million believers by 2030."

Chamonix, happy and tanned, worked for the National Trust and was sitting on the ground next to a sign, far out on the Lizard peninsula, painting its embossed metal letters black.

Her work was interesting and varied, maintaining the Trust's paths, steps and signs.

Trevor was a professor, in his seventies, who was out for a cliff walk to help deal with the recent loss of dear friends.

I'M NO SHAKESPEARE

Trevor was keen to chat.

He shared his deep concern about climate change and the negative effect humans are having on the planet.

He was convinced that Artificial Intelligence, on its trawl through all available evidence, would come to the unequivocal conclusion that humans were the greatest threat to the planet, and thus humans would begin to be eliminated by machines.

We ended our conversation on a lighter note by both observing the clouds, perfectly fluffy, white on top with a dark grey base.

We agreed that they were the clouds that in school we had both been taught how to paint.

I eventually arrived at the Lizard and camped at Henry's camping.

It had been another long day, twenty three km of walking, made more challenging by high temperatures and the need to drink double my usual amount of water.

Thirty five years of postnatal bladder training have been undone in five weeks.

Like a dog who can last all night in a house, and in the morning be taken on a lead along the pavement, only to urinate as soon as its paws touch grass, so has my bladder considered the coast path as Carnival time.

In this energy sapping heat, even with a significantly increased fluid intake, bladder output is still reduced.

Dehydration is something to avoid at all costs, and adequate hydration needs to be carefully managed.

I'M NO SHAKESPEARE

It had been at least a week since my last rest day, and with a fish and chip shop, an ice cream shop, and a pub all within two minutes walking distance of Henry's, an easy decision was made.

To stay for two nights.

DAY 37

Dingo Den

My plan was to stroll, without my backpack, to the Lizard lighthouse.

There was, however, no escape from domestic tasks, and I had some particularly unpleasant laundry to deal with.

On a campsite, laundry needs to be babysat, like a watched pot that never boils.

At Henry's there was one covered area, the Dingo Den, full of scattered old sofas and armchairs, and free range chickens scratching in wood chippings.

It was the only place on the site that had any WiFi.

I joined the teenagers who were sprawled everywhere, one girl sobbing loudly over her excellent A level results.

This campsite was a strange and wonderful place, with sculpted wood figures, and animal enclosures.

Ducks and cockerels roused campers at the crack of dawn.

I'M NO SHAKESPEARE

Hand painted murals, randomly placed granite sinks, colourful geodesic tiles, and ground embedded bottles added to this visual antithesis to the traditional farmer's field camp site.

The toilet cubicles were separated by sheets of corrugated metal, while late into the evening soft classic music played throughout the wash block.

Mature bushes and bright flowers grew everywhere, and in the evening concealed lighting in the foliage, lamps, and strings of fairy lights created a magical atmosphere.

The entire site appeared to have been a work of art born of the psychedelic hallucinations of a completely stoned hippy.

While I had been laundering, a sea fog had descended, and the eerie blasts of an intermittent horn began to sound from the Lizard lighthouse station.

They were sending a warning to all shipping, to steer clear of the treacherous Lizard coast and its underwater reefs, where in any rough weather, shipping is advised to keep at least three miles offshore.

The Lizard peninsula protrudes so far into the Channel that it is the biggest ship trap in British waters.

Like a siren call however, the horn was luring me back to the coast path, where its sound was loudest.

I returned, via Roskilly's for a double scoop of clotted cream vanilla with a flake and extra clotted cream, to where I had left the path the day before.

After a total of eight km walking around the Lizard Point, lighthouse, Housel Bay, lifeboat and coastguard stations, I made my way from Church Cove back inland to Henry's.

I'M NO SHAKESPEARE

And it was from Church Cove that I planned to restart the coast path the following morning.

I would be walking for just eight more days before temporarily leaving the path, to fulfil a commitment to provide two weeks of home respite care for a very dear ninety nine year old gentleman.

I needed to earn some money, to maintain my cooked breakfast and local beer tasting habits.

Transitioning into early Autumn I would need to upgrade both my camping mattress and my sleeping bag.

These cold dewy nights, likely soon to become frosty, were no longer comfortable with my existing kit.

Once the cold dampness had penetrated my right hip, the resulting dull ache would last until dawn.

I did not want to spend a small fortune on an ultralight four season mattress, so I intended to try what Chris had suggested, which was to lay an emergency first aid silver space blanket under my inflatable mattress.

If that failed, and I half hoped it might, then a medicinal brandy may need to be added to my bedtime routine.

I also considered adding a lightweight down camping quilt to my down sleeping bag, to be used flexibly alongside my current bag inside bivy combination.

The strength I had gained from five weeks of walking meant that I should not have too much difficulty adding a little extra weight to my pack.

DAY 38

Fog Horn

The fog horn, which was operated automatically by a fog detector, sounded every thirty seconds throughout the night.

I had found its regularity soothing, and had enjoyed falling asleep to the deep, low vibrations.

In the wash block, however, I overheard some bleary eyed campers cursing it in the familiar way that I have been known to curse trying to sleep with a snorer.

As I approached Church Cove from Lizard village the fog grew thicker.

The sea could be heard but was not visible.

I thought of the ship's Captains, of them hearing the warning blasts of the fog horn, but the shore remaining dangerously invisible.

After an hour of walking, the fog began to clear.

White wisps blew up over the cliffs from the sea, and a faded ball of light began to appear in the sky.

I'M NO SHAKESPEARE

Serpentine is an attractive, naturally formed stone, named after its likeness to the texture of a snake's skin, and is part of the Earth's mantle pushed up to the surface.

It is found on the Lizard peninsula and polishes to a beautiful shine, its lustre obvious underfoot, especially in places rubbed by repeated footsteps.

Richard has a workshop in Lizard village where he produces beautiful jewellery made of serpentine stone.

We chatted and laughed for a while about our similar experiences of having travelled and lived in Eastern Europe.

On the way to Kennack Sands I passed the ruins of what was once a thriving Victorian factory.

A large waterwheel had provided the power for constructing mantle pieces, gravestones, shop fronts, and polished ornaments from the local serpentine stone quarried nearby.

An information sign states that in 1883 twenty men and three boys had been employed there.

I met a local woman who was walking her dog on the cliffs.

She was originally from a city in Devon, but had fallen in love with a fisherman and had lived in a small fishing village on the Lizard for over thirty years.

We compared the anonymity of city living, to that of village life, where everyone knows, or supposes, or invents, everyone else's business.

In Kennack Sands two happy ladies working in a beach cafe prepared for me a 'turbo' cooked breakfast.

"We won't let you go hungry!" one of them said, with a wink.

I'M NO SHAKESPEARE

As she cooked, she recounted to me how living in Devonport, Plymouth, in the late eighties, was like living "in the Bronx".

Another storm was approaching and I was keen to make quick headway towards Coverack, which was my planned destination.

I arrived and rested in the harbour pub, and using the pub wifi I discovered a campsite further out towards St. Keverne.

Roskilly's ice cream farm campsite was ideally located, exactly on the inland path detour that was currently in place due to quarry work around Porthoustock.

A phone call confirmed my pitch for the evening and, refreshed, I set off to walk for another two hours, whilst the storm chased and overtook me.

Sadly, after pitching in torrential rain and heavy wind, I was far too cold and wet for ice cream.

A quiet corner sofa of the tea room was where I hid out, until closing time at 2030, and cuddled a pot of hot tea.

As I was walking back across the field towards my tent I was called over to join two couples, friends from Cornwall, who were sitting at the communal table in the camping field's covered area.

They were drinking prosecco, eating hummus and garlic biscuits, and laughing defiantly whilst Storm Betty raged around them.

Staying in dry, heated camper vans, they were displaying significantly more bravado than I was.

However, after a lovely time and a tipsy crawl into my sleeping bag, my usual age related night time internal combustion engine allowed me to sleep well and warmly.

DAY 39

Half way

The next morning, on the road to Porthallow, I was drenched by another heavy shower.

The staff at the Fat Apples cafe, just before the village, kindly found me a warm indoor table, where I ordered coffee and a cooked breakfast, and waited for the rain to pass.

On Porthallow beach there stands a sculpture to mark the exact halfway point of the South West Coast Path, three hundred and fifteen miles.

Porthallow is a fishing village that time forgot, and also holds happy holiday memories for me.

Our son, James, was five years old and our daft water loving spaniel, who infuriatingly used to race into the sea up to her knees and then refuse to return, was six months old.

We spent a week in an old fisherman's cottage in Porthallow, together with Franzi, our Summer au pair from Germany.

With John and I both working twenty four hour shifts, frequent unplanned overtime or overruns, and with the older children having

I'M NO SHAKESPEARE

already left home for work and study, we hosted au pairs to help take care of James.

In Porthallow with Franzi we played an alternative game of Scrabble, where the only rule was that the words had to 'sound' German.

Basically, any old combination of letters was acceptable.

It was hard to believe that I had just walked three hundred and fifteen miles, and over such difficult terrain, and was now standing in that same village.

I was asked last night whether walking the path was not monotonous.

I replied simply, "Oh no, never!"

Today, while walking, I considered a deeper answer to this question, for which I was completely unprepared.

There are certainly the same tasks each day, to take down and to erect my tent.

My legs move in the same rhythmic way every day, one step at a time, covering an average of twenty km, and I carry my heavy pack for up to ten hours.

Like everyone, I have daily requirements for food, drink, and hygiene.

But on no day does the sea, the sky or even the ground, appear exactly like on any other.

As I walk, every second of every day is unique, different shadows and light, clouds, weather, seasons, learning about geology, human and natural history, insects, birds, trees, buildings.

I'M NO SHAKESPEARE

The physical challenge, problem solving, the freedom of my thoughts.

The people I meet on the path or in the Inns, cafes, campsites, and hostels.

Having the time to walk any long distance trail is a privilege, and to me has honestly never felt monotonous.

I have a Bulgarian friend who is the head of a European frontier border crossing point, between Bulgaria and Turkey.

He tells me that every day, groups of desperate people, mostly men, only because the journey is so hard and dangerous, travel by foot, many from Afghanistan, to try to get to Europe.

They carry just small bags with water and some food, and do not have cutting edge or ultralight hiking gear.

Their risks are huge, and at the borders they are hunted like animals by police with dogs.

Every day I think of them and of how my little walk, in comparison to theirs, is just a personal indulgence.

My evening was spent in a simply wonderful campsite in Maenporth, looking down like a Queen onto a field full of large family tents, awnings, caravans and camper vans.

At Tregedna Farm a 'Rambler's Rest' had been thoughtfully designed and set aside for the exclusive use of hikers.

It included a magnificent, raised, three walled, wooden room, with a vaulted roof, balcony, table, and bench.

I had arrived, exhausted, after a twenty five km walk around the Gillian river estuary, to the warmest welcome ever given from any campsite.

I'M NO SHAKESPEARE

"You have all come such a long way by foot that we want to give you somewhere special."

DAY 40

Our Country's Moat

I slept like a log, safe in the hug of my Rambler's Rest, and needed extra face splashes of cold water to wake me up.

I stopped early for a strong coffee and a sausage bap at Swanpool beach, and then headed off to Falmouth to catch two ferries, firstly to St. Mawes, and then to Place on the Roseland peninsula.

On the path towards Falmouth I spotted a metal bench in front of a thought provoking and poetically engraved monument.

"For freedom

This seat and the path leading thereto have been provided as a memorial to the men of number 11 falmouth, company of the home guard who during 1940. 41. 42. 43. 44. After their day's work nightly patrolled this coast, armed and vigilant against german landings.

Thus they watched 1000 dawns appear across these great waters which form our country's moat."

I wondered whether we would be so hostile towards other small boats if people could walk between France and England in the same

I'M NO SHAKESPEARE

way as they walk between Germany and France, with no geographical barrier, with no such 'moat', which we like to claim as ours and even arrogantly call the 'English' Channel.

On the first ferry, to St. Mawes, I met an inspiring couple, who were on holiday in Falmouth, and were both experienced long distance walkers.

Their next planned adventure would be to walk the Corfu Trail, and they asked interesting questions about my journey, including wanting to know what was my 'most useful' and my 'I wish I had brought' kit.

Raf was a very chatty and cheerful skipper from Poland, who stood proudly at the helm of the St. Mawes to Place ferry.

He had arrived in the UK as a teenager, not understanding any spoken English, but he now speaks like a real Cornishman.

He told me that he had recently bought his own second hand wooden boat.

She was still nameless, but after some love and attention, when her true character starts to shine, he will name her.

In Falmouth there is a plaque on a bench that reads:

Into the sunshine

John Charles Barnett

Simply the best husband, father, grandfather

Loved to infinity and beyond

In the blink of an eye (metaphorically speaking, because I do know how babies are made), John and I had also become grandparents.

I'M NO SHAKESPEARE

Our twin granddaughters had recently been born.

My John, who is also a truly wonderful husband, father and grandfather, and who does, frequently, drive me to insanity and beyond, had flown to the UK to help with the twins.

He was giving emotional and hands on support to his daughter, and to his son in law, but was inexplicably sending me photographs of car seats, pushchairs, and lawn mowers.

For the last mile into Portscatho I walked with Steven, who was also an experienced coast path walker, and we compared our experiences of different sections of the path.

Steven, a local Crown prosecutor with a logical mind, and a sharp attention to detail, was an excellent conversation partner.

After a good meal and a pint in the local pub, and as the Aperol Yachties started to became louder, I decided to walk on and away from Portscatho.

I found a wild camp, high above Pendower beach, where I hoped to sleep undisturbed until dawn.

DAY 41

Cappuccino

"Cappuccino, signora?"

I looked up into Giovanni's smiling, liquid brown eyes as he placed his warm hand on my shoulder.

Was I dreaming, or was I really being cooked bacon and eggs, with toast, marmalade, and real butter, by a gorgeous Italian man on a cottage terrace overlooking Portloe harbour?

At dawn, in the still and bird song of the early morning, and leaving no trace, I had dismantled my camp.

At a bench approaching Nare Head I had prepared coffee.

By the time I reached Portloe, having been an ignored shepherdess to two escaped sheep, unable to find their way back to their babies, I was more than ready for a cooked breakfast.

I asked a smiling couple, hand in hand and out for a morning stroll, if there might be a cafe in the village.

Disappointingly there was not, and it was too early for the pub to be offering food.

I'M NO SHAKESPEARE

Annie and Giovanni, who live together overlooking the harbour, insisted I go and wait for them on the wooden rocking seat in their garden.

"Over there, with the orange windows. Giovanni will cook for you!" Annie ordered.

And that is how I found myself being treated, listening once again to the wonderful sound of the Italian language, the sea lapping gently against the harbour beach, trying my hardest to remember my table manners, and sipping the most delicious cappuccino this side of Italy.

After saying a humble and heartfelt thank you to them both, I continued towards Gorran Haven, and almost stepped on an adder, laying in wait, lengthways, along the centre of the path.

On a bed of broken bracken leaves, the zigzags along its back afforded a perfect camouflage.

If I had not seen it first, I would surely have stepped on it.

With my heart thumping, I stood motionless, scanning the ground in all directions around me for any other members of this adder family who might be nearby.

As I began to calm, I took some photographs and, not taking my eyes from the snake, who was also watching me, I sidled past.

Having seen nobody on the path for several kilometres, I called out a warning to a teenage girl who, at that same moment, was walking towards me, concentrating on her telephone and paying no attention to where she was placing her feet.

At Treveague Farm, Gorran Haven, I was directed to the hiker's area in the far top corner of the furthest away field.

I'M NO SHAKESPEARE

I was assured that this was because it was quiet and traffic free, and not because we smell.

Shortly after my arrival, another lone hiker, similarly dispatched, trudged up to join me.

Sarah was walking, at a fast pace, to Land's End, with a great optimism and sense of adventure, and she became an instant friend.

DAY 42

Anthony

I was woken, not by Sarah, who had already sped silently off towards Falmouth by the time I emerged from my tent, but by the warmth of the morning sun.

My last day of walking had coincided with a perfect summer day, and I wanted to savour every second, starting with a bacon bap from the campsite restaurant.

At Gorran Haven I rested on a bench in the town, overlooking the beach.

Sophie, my age, was on holiday and had been bathing with an early morning sea swimming group.

She had prepared a mug of coffee in her holiday cottage, a stone's throw from the bench, and was now relaxing there and drinking her coffee.

We chatted for more than an hour, and Sophie told me that she cared for her mother and had a teenage son, that she loved reading travel books, and that she dreamed of the day when she too would be free to walk.

I'M NO SHAKESPEARE

Gorran Haven was the second place for me, after Marazion that evoked a strong feeling of 'I could live here'.

Arriving in Mevagissey and feeling extremely thirsty, I entered the oldest pub in the narrowest street.

For more than the cost of two pints of beer, I ordered two chilled bottles of Appletiser, and carried them outside to join Anthony, a marvellously eccentric old sailor, on a wooden bench in the shaded cool of the narrow street.

Anthony held me in open-mouthed awe, riveted by his tales of daring on the seven seas.

He was a rule breaking bad boy, but sensitive and intelligent, totally charming, and had sailed from France to scatter his parent's ashes at sea in Pentewan bay.

Their ashes had been travelling in his cockpit for far too long, and Anthony had eventually decided that Pentewan Bay was to be their final resting place.

It was where he, as a boy, remembered having enjoyed the best ever family holiday.

There was a poignancy to Anthony's story, not only for him, but also for me.

It was in a camping field in the Pentewan Valley, thirty three years ago, that I met and fell in love with another eccentric man.

Over twenty years older than me, Bernard, a Cornish farmer whose grandfather had been a tin miner, had seduced me with his home grown tomatoes.

I'M NO SHAKESPEARE

Bernard has since died, but our son, who was born thirty one years ago, would be waiting for me with my grandchildren when I arrived at Pentewan beach.

Anthony and I hugged each other and, with a lump in my throat, I continued towards my family.

The Pause Between Walking

After forty days and forty nights of feasting rather than of fasting, and of very earthy pleasures, my Pyramid was retired, and my sleeping bag and socks gratefully laundered.

In the pause between my walking, I cared for a ninety nine year old man, who for his ninetieth birthday had enjoyed a flying lesson.

His life had once been so independent, full of work and action, and now, although completely dependent on others, his life was no less precious, and it was a privilege to care for him.

I missed carrying my home on my back, and the coolness of grass scented breeze on my sleeping face.

I missed my husband.

Occasionally.

And I missed the sea.

But the gentle daily routines of caring gave me time to reflect.

Before I took my first step from the bus at Minehead, I had questioned my physical ability.

I'M NO SHAKESPEARE

The heavy weight of my backpack had upset my balance, and I had been acutely aware of the pressure in my feet, and nervous of the blisters that I was certain would soon appear.

I had doubted my stamina and resolve.

By comparison to then, the weight of my backpack now felt familiar, even comforting.

My sense of balance had adjusted quickly, and my core strength increased rapidly.

I had never before used walking poles, and at first I was uncoordinated.

Six weeks later I was planting them with the precision of an Olympic baton twirler, and felt naked without them.

They had helped me balance on uneven ground, and had relieved pressure through my knees.

Covering blisters with good quality plasters, and releasing fluid where necessary, had helped them heal quickly with minimal discomfort.

The skin on the soles of my feet had noticeably hardened, which made new blisters less likely.

I was still careful to wear dry socks wherever possible, and I immediately removed any grit and smoothed any ridged areas that might appear in my double layered socks.

I frequently adjusted my shoe laces to keep my feet held firmly.

At the end of each day I would hobble, due to carrying so much weight for so many kms, and my feet, knees and hips would become stiff and painful after even the shortest rest.

I'M NO SHAKESPEARE

After stopping walking, the stiffness and pain lingered, and my muscles and tendons took their time to recover.

Other than when my tibialis tendonitis was at its most acute, I had not taken any pain relief or anti-inflammatory medicine.

Mentally my stamina and resolve had not wavered, with a high calorie diet and careful hydration being crucial to maintaining my energy levels.

I think that by choosing to walk slowly, my body and mind had been placed under the least possible amount of stress, and I had remained motivated, even on the wettest, coldest days.

I have already described how the benefits of my experiences far outweighed any physical discomfort.

Additionally, there were more personal reasons that made quitting completely unthinkable.

One of my younger sisters had lived with Motor Neurone Disease, and in the last two years of her life she became unable to walk, to scratch an itch, or finally to breathe.

My other sister would dearly have liked to walk, but she had recently undergone major, life changing, surgery.

I walked because they could not, and so to give up was never an option.

I walked too for the twenty seven year old me, who thirty years ago had tried to walk the path, but had had to give up.

And I walked for the ninety nine year old me, who I suspected would have been my biggest cheerleader.

In the ambulance service self reflection was important.

I'M NO SHAKESPEARE

We were encouraged to write our observations and critical evaluations, as a personal learning tool.

I have one overriding observation.

To slow down.

For the second half of my walk, and for the second half of my life, I would like to be less focused on each daily destination.

I would like to take even more time to sit on benches, both real and metaphorical.

Because, less than a week after my walk, everything that was a vivid stream of reality, has separated into snapshots.

Frustrating gaps have appeared, and it is impossible to remember the names and order of every cove, each sensation, and every human encounter.

On the path, I met many walkers who were trying to cover ground as quickly as possible, and who, in one day, would walk as many kms as I would walk in two days.

Their speed was often applauded by others.

I think about the end of their journey, and the end of my old man's journey, and I wonder about memory gaps, and whether they too, like me, come to regret their speed.

DAY 43

Hypoglycemia

We were back at Pentewan Sands.

"Mum!"

"You look like a rag and bone man with all that stuff dangling off you?!"

It was a Sunday morning and I was sitting with my daughter, Carly, who despite having laughed at my appearance had just complained of a stitch simply walking from the tent to the cafe.

We had arrived and camped at Pentewan the previous evening, and we were almost ready to start walking.

But first, in the holiday park restaurant, a Full Cornish …

"Mum!"

"You are not allowed to have a full cooked breakfast"

"Not until you have earned it!"

My daughter is a reception teacher, and she can be quite bossy.

I'M NO SHAKESPEARE

Carly also taught in Germany for five years, which might explain her bizarre breakfast rules.

I was thrilled that she was sharing my first day back on the path, so I quietly accepted my permitted breakfast of half a pancake and a handful of fresh blueberries.

It was a perfect morning and we set off, at my usual gentle pace, laughing and chatting.

The sea was calm and flat, and there were many canoeists, snorkelers, and paddle boarders enjoying the safe conditions.

The land ahead, according to a red faced man who came panting towards us, sounded far more dangerous, and full of what he warned us were 'killer steps'.

And it was just before Porthpean, possibly in part due to the killer steps, that my blood sugars started to nose dive.

"Mum!"

Apparently I was waving my poles in an alarmingly uncoordinated way, and talking to blackberries.

Neither of which are entirely out of character.

But, as I had also started to feel quite wobbly and light headed, we sat down immediately in the middle of a sheep field and prepared emergency spicy cous cous.

Feeling heaps better I picked up my pace.

"Mum!"

"Slow down!"

"You're very reactive to food!"

I'M NO SHAKESPEARE

Then, upon reaching the beach cafe at Porthpean, I was delighted to learn that, like a sticker or extra playground time, we had both earned a double scoop of strawberry clotted cream ice cream.

We parted at Charlestown harbour after a crafty tapping together of my poles and slurred rendition of "I am the music man" had earned me an extra slice of lemon and raspberry polenta, and I continued alone past the pink shorts and shirts of the golfers at Carlyon Bay.

On the path beside the Carlyon Bay hotel I passed a bench, on which there was a plaque to Terry Bradley, who had obviously known a thing or two about basic survival on the coast path:

In memory of Terry Radley

Rest in peace dad, enjoy the view

We'll come here often with your beloved grandchildren and plenty of sweets xxx

Kelly was my age, and worked in a hotel in Fowey.

She stopped me to chat as I was walking through the dusty pavements of Par.

I detected a South African accent, and asked her what she was doing living in Par of all places, which was about as far away from the majesty, colour, scent, and sounds of South Africa as it was physically possible to be.

"Oh I ask myself that every day" she replied.

"I need to leave but have only just learned to drive".

I really hoped she would make it out.

I'M NO SHAKESPEARE

At Par I camped in a pub garden, from where I cruelly interrupted my daughter's lesson planning by calling to ask her advice on what I should order from the menu.

I fell asleep feeling indescribably wonderful to be back walking again.

DAY 44

Hannibal

"You are the first real walker we have met so far today, and you look very ... um ... organized!"

Exclaimed a retired couple as we passed each other on my way from Par to Fowey.

I was still basking in having been described as 'organised' rather than 'rag and bone', when I met a lone male at Gribbin Head, raw whortleberry juice running down his chin.

Hannibal was walking straight towards me, carrying what appeared to be a sawn off shotgun.

It was the way he was holding his rolled up beach towel along his arm, more than any glinting gunmetal, that caught my attention, as if it was disguising something.

I was immediately on guard and, in the interests of national security, and my own nosiness, I challenged him.

"Where is your husband?" he immediately demanded.

I'M NO SHAKESPEARE

Like asking a child where their parents are, but with far more menace.

The hairs on the back of my neck twitched.

I answered assertively that my husband was right behind me, with our very protective German Shepherd.

I pulled my emergency whistle out of my fanny pack and gave it a few earsplitting blasts before striding briskly away.

Once safely away, and across the river from Fowey to Polruan, I honoured my resolution to slow down and I stopped, after just five hours of walking, at a campsite with panoramic views of the sea

In a local pub that evening I sketched photofits of shotgun man on the back of napkins while waiting for my telephone to charge.

Once my telephone was fully charged I was attracted by a Facebook advert, and I booked myself an exciting upcoming day off.

I would be putting my feet up, and eating my body weight in delicious French food, on a cheap over and back cruise deal to France, from Plymouth to Roscoff, with Brittany Ferries.

DAY 45

Doberman Church

The dawn air, with its musky scent of fresh grass, damp earth and cattle, blew softly against my resting face.

The evenings may have been getting darker and cooler but, cocooned snugly in my additional down quilt, I had been sleeping well and warmly.

It was a crisp, sunny September morning when I met Ronald, a fit and kind, retired gentleman, walking towards me on the path from Polruan to Polperro.

Originally from Surrey, Ronald had retired to Polruan, to his dream house with a sun room overlooking the sea, and from where he walked the coast path each day.

We had a fascinating chat about spectacles, and about Ronald's previous career which had included organising the very first flamboyant international hairdressing exhibitions in the 60's.

Ronald told me that each day on returning home from his daily walk, he lies down, like "Lionel Messi", to allow his body time to recover.

I'M NO SHAKESPEARE

I understood the need for rest and recovery at the end of each of my long days of walking, and loved Ronald's scientific sounding 'Lionel Messi' for horizontal time.

I stowed it away for future reference, to substitute for 'lazy'.

Ronald was widowed, and smiled as he told me that his wife had also been called Cheryl.

Before we parted he gave me detailed directions to his favorite wild swimming cove.

"Keep an eye out", he said, using another of his unique descriptions.

"For the church that looks like a Doberman".

The beaches on this section of the path were a wild swimmer's dream, and I stripped off eagerly to swim in the calm sea at the easily accessible Parsons cove.

From their position sitting on the rocks at the back of the beach, a sizeable group of American hikers watched me.

I waved to them, as I picked my way barefooted over the pebbles, trying my best to at least hold good posture in my big pants and sports bra.

Determined to not show any less than British reaction to the cold water, I plunged straight in, bit my stiff upper lip, and grimaced as I waited for the cold shock to give way to the pleasure and freedom of being back in the sea.

Behind me, on the beach, a dog was being yelled at by its owners.

I'M NO SHAKESPEARE

Elvis the terrier was running in delighted circles, shaking something in its mouth that, without my spectacles, I could not be totally sure was not one of my socks.

Thankfully both socks remained intact and, after dressing and tying my wet underwear to my backpack to be dried as I walked, I climbed back to the path, where I set to preparing hot chocolate beside a bench.

Gertrude, my age, a feisty Swiss redhead, was also walking from Minehead to Poole.

She stopped brusquely to chat, even more brusquely.

Gertrude prefers to stay in hotels along the path rather than to camp, and rattled off all the things she dislikes about the UK, including the disgusting way that we treat our dogs like children.

I told her that some even treat their dogs as mega rock stars, but she wasn't listening.

Gertrude was on her third pair of boots since Minehead.

We met, and even walked together, a few more times during our respective journeys to Poole, and I came to understand why her poor boots kept choosing to self-destruct.

In Polperro, after a meal in a harbour pub, I continued wearily to a farm campsite, a short but very steep hill walk away from the village.

In the tent next to mine a young french couple were chatting softly and I strained to eavesdrop on their conversation, excited that I would soon be practicing French again, even if only for a day.

That evening, before sleep, my excitement turned to sadness.

I'M NO SHAKESPEARE

From his daughter I had received a message to inform me that my dear ninety nine year old client had died.

DAY 46

Ship Tracker Jo

Rising early after a fitful sleep I retraced my steps down the steep hill into Polperro, and stopped at a sunny outdoor cafe for an extended breakfast.

Coffee and a bacon and sausage bap, and a friendly chat with some day walkers, helped to lift my spirits.

The path between Polperro and Looe was a popular tourist route, and was especially busy on such a glorious sunny day.

I chatted with several more happy and relaxed walkers, including Len and Dierdre, who were retired, but who had once employed Bulgarians in their UK potato producing business.

I was proud to hear their great praise for the hard work, good manners, and intelligence of their old Bulgarian employees, and I experienced my first real homesickness for my adopted country.

At Talland Bay while resting at another cafe terrace and drinking tea, I remembered how it was at this exact spot, thirty years ago, that my son and I had been rescued by a kind dog walker who had offered us her friend's garden in which to camp.

I'M NO SHAKESPEARE

The years slip by imperceptibly, and so too does youthful strength.

Walking onwards towards Looe I asked myself how I had ever managed to carry a heavy pack, plus my son, for such a distance and over such tough terrain.

But what I may have lost in raw power, I had perhaps gained in stamina, and most certainly in appetite.

I reached Looe, starving, and headed immediately to a fish and chip shop.

There I met Ship Tracker Jo, a postie my age from Bude.

Jo was single and regularly travels for weekend and holiday adventures in Bambi, her adored old camper van.

By chance we shared a table in the fish and chip cafe, immediately became best friends and confidants, and decided to retire to the pub opposite the chippy and to share a beer.

I learned that one of Jo's friends, Henry, was also by chance going to be sailing on Friday evening on the same overnight ferry crossing as me, to France from Plymouth.

Henry would be heading in his camper van to Biarritz, and the most crucial detail of all was that he would have a cabin, with a shower.

Jo immediately messaged him with a photograph of me, head buff neatly straightened to cover my wild hair, and lifting my pint coquettishly to the camera in what I quite believed to be a warm and friendly greeting.

She introduced me to Henry as her new vagrant friend, and asked if he might allow me a shower in his cabin.

I'M NO SHAKESPEARE

The answer came back without delay:

"No F****** chance!"

Bambi was parked on a site at Millendreath, beyond Looe, and as it sounded to be an ideal camping location for me too, we walked there together, stopping at the beach for another beer before climbing a steep lane to the site.

I paid my ten pounds to pitch alongside Bambi, then we shared lemon cheesecake and a cup of tea, and Jo showed me her ship tracker app.

Like a game of Top Trumps, pictures and statistics are displayed when a telephone is pointed towards any ship of any size.

Nationality, type, age, origin and destination, speed or whether at anchor.

It was marvelously addictive and I couldn't wait to download my own ship tracker app.

It reminded of an app I used to have for identifying dog breeds, but had lost all trust in after pointing it at my husband and learning that I was married to a Labrador.

DAY 47

Plymouth

For some incomprehensible reason, Jo attributed her phobia of porridge to having once kept horses.

Over breakfast, at the shared wooden picnic bench beside Bambi, she had looked across with barely disguised disgust at my all-purpose mug of slimy oats.

The semi instant porridge was designed to be microwaved, but in the absence of a microwave my habit was simply to add boiling water and to leave to stand.

We checked out the statistics of a large ship in the bay, that had been completely lit from bow to stern all night, and that had not moved.

It was thrillingly revealed to be a Maltese warship at anchor.

Jo and I said goodbye to each other, and I set off walking again, through a woodland and across a freshly cut hay field, towards Seaton.

As I descended the steep hill to approach the beach at Seaton, a familiar aroma wafted up the cliff road towards me.

I'M NO SHAKESPEARE

It was all the persuasion I needed to stop at the busy beach cafe, and to order my second breakfast.

Nearing Portwrinkle I met David, my age, who was resting on the first bench for several miles.

He scooted up chivalrously to make space for me, and we chatted.

David was out on a several day hike of the path with a group of seven others.

Their day's destination was to be in the comfort of the Edgecumbe Arms pub on the Cornish side of the Tamar river.

My own rather more loose plan for the day was to find a wild camp somewhere near the Rame peninsula.

I had not slept well for two consecutive nights, due to the sad news of my client's death, and the previous night because of the owls that had been hooting loudly above my tent.

Covering thirty two km, to reach Plymouth, seemed ambitious.

David was also a carer, and a kind and empathetic man.

He had lost his group, perhaps deliberately, and was enjoying walking solo.

I left him lost in his own thoughts on the bench, and soon found myself traversing the Portwrinkle golf course and heading towards the red flags of Tregantle firing range.

A group of golfers at the closest tee to the coast path gate to the firing ranges warned me not to continue any further.

I'M NO SHAKESPEARE

They pointed officiously with their clubs, telling me to walk past several more greens towards the road, which they assured me was the only alternative route if I did not want to get shot at.

What ensued was a circumnavigation of the course, a stealth wee beside the furthest green, and some frustrated cursing.

It was proving impossible to escape this open air prison where the guards, or perhaps the inmates, all wore pink shorts or pink shirts.

I eventually clambered over a padlocked five bar gate to reach a pavement that ran alongside the road that bypassed the red flagged area.

After a short while my curses turned to a more grateful type of blasphemy when I spied a pub car park.

A packet of crisps and a pint later, I was refreshed, rested, and ready to continue the long road trudge towards Whitsand Bay and past the wooden cabins and chalets that are haphazardly dotted along its cliffs.

Spotting an ice cream van in a car park elicited further unrestrained whoops of joy and I ordered a very expensive but totally worth it double cone with two flakes and extra clotted cream.

"Ooo, I don't sell many of them!" the ice cream van man exclaimed.

As always, the sight of a headland, in this case Rame Head, spurred me on, curious and impatient for the coastline of the next bay to be revealed.

It was then a dark and eerie walk through the woods of Mt. Edgecumbe Country Park at dusk.

I'M NO SHAKESPEARE

My legs and feet were aching, but I had already almost completed the entire distance to Plymouth that I had earlier believed to be beyond my capability.

I was relieved to emerge from the spookiness into the open formal grass gardens and Orangery areas of the park.

The Cremyll ferry, for foot passengers only, was patiently waiting at the jetty to carry me across the Tamar River, to the bright lights of the large and noisy city of Plymouth.

DAY 48

Night Crossing

A day off after such exertion, and the nurture of my mother and of her cooking, was very sorely needed.

Stepping out of bed, after a night of sweet slumber on what continues, after fifty years, to be the most comfortable mattress I have ever slept on, I hobbled to the bathroom and stood for a long, long while under a powerfully hot and steamy shower.

The previous evening, from the ferry steps on the Plymouth side of the Tamar River, I had been scooped up by my mother.

I was now in her warm and comfortable home, in the town of Ivybridge on the edge of Dartmoor, eleven miles from the city.

My one set of clothes had been quickly laundered and, as it had been almost six weeks since Nafa had so expertly cut my hair in Newquay, I hoped I may find a similar no-nonsense service in Ivybridge.

The pavement billboard and wall photographs depicted solely male models, and the barber nearest to the door appeared to be in the process of cutting a man's throat.

I'M NO SHAKESPEARE

He made a further attempt to put me off by saying that he could not cut my hair unless I wanted a man's style.

I smiled, shrugged, and took a seat.

In fact I was thrilled with his no fuss, skilled work, which cost less than half of the price of a 'female' hairdressing salon.

A relaxed and gentle day was then shared with my mother before she drove me, my backpack, and my poles, to the ferry port, from where I was to sail on the overnight cross channel ferry to France.

My gas canister was confiscated by the preboarding security search, but I was soon on board and laying out my foam mat and down quilt in a secluded space in the quiet reclining chair lounge area.

Like the white noise app I sometimes use to block out the sound of John's snoring, the deep vibrations of the great engines soon lulled me into slumber.

Cradled too by the gentle roll of the ferry, and with just a handful of sleepy sock-footed wanders out into the cool air of the poop deck, I slept warmly and peacefully.

DAY 49

Roscoff

The sexy French accented tannoy announcement at 0700 was my hypnotic svengali to head to the onboard cafe.

With my newly shorn hair sticking out in all directions I must have resembled an orphaned ostrich as I lurched, with each roll of the ship, along the main corridor to the cafe.

A familiar looking man was lurching towards me.

"Henry!" I squealed excitedly.

"How was your cabin?"

Henry looked at me blankly, so I continued:

"I'm Cheryl! Jo's great unwashed friend!"

A horrified realization dawned as he stuttered a nervous "Oh. Yeah. Um. Hi."

He then bolted down to the vehicle deck, to no doubt lock himself inside his campervan.

I wanted to make the most of every available second before docking, to eat as much typically French breakfast as possible.

I'M NO SHAKESPEARE

So I chose a strong black coffee, a fresh orange juice, two buttery croissants, and a baguette with butter and strawberry jam.

My early morning walk down to the small and sleepy granite town of Roscoff afforded wide views across the wild and rocky bays where the tidal ranges are some of the fastest and widest in Europe.

I visited the harbour and then continued through the town towards the beaches, practicing a few "bonjours" and "votre chien est tres beau" with impossibly chic looking dog walkers.

It started to rain, a fine French drizzle, so I bought a copy of Le Monde and sat in a cafe where I read, drank more coffee, attempted, stickily, to delicately eat an apricot pastry, and pretended to be French.

The piece de la resistance of my Gallic day off was a lazy lunch of moules frites and red wine at a pavement restaurant.

The feast was topped off with a dessert of Breton tiramisu made with caramelized apples, creme brulé and toasted almonds, and a sweet dessert wine.

On my walk back to the ferry port to check in for my late afternoon return sailing, I entered a small supermarket to buy some extra mature camembert and red wine as a present for my adult son.

I also chose an authentic stripey Breton top from a clothes shop, as a birthday present for my "petite fille", my granddaughter, who would soon be celebrating her third birthday

It had been raining heavily in Plymouth, not fine French drizzle, but mucky Cornish mizzle, and the disembarking took longer than usual.

By the time all the foot passengers had cleared customs there were no remaining taxis.

I'M NO SHAKESPEARE

As I had not really stopped eating all day, I began to walk, hood up, through the horrors of Plymouth's Saturday evening club land.

Carrying my pack, and extra grateful for the protection of my poles, I wove past rowdy drunken groups, and attracted unwanted attention from street beggars.

Eventually, having passed safely through the red light district and the night club areas, I reached the commercial city centre and a row of black cabs.

My son, and Cooper, his large, black, rescue German Shepherd, were waiting for me at their small flat not far from the city centre.

Cooper howled like a wolf at the shadowy figure standing in the kitchen.

A figure with a humped back, two big sticks, and stinking, like an old sock, of extra mature Camembert.

Cooper was immediately upgraded to share his master's bedroom, and I went to my mat in the living room.

DAY 50

Ferryman

A Sunday morning and another day of heavy rain and wind.

Yet another storm had started and was expected to bring even stronger, gale force, winds within the next few days.

The prospect of continuing to walk from Plymouth, especially after having experienced some French high life, seemed less and less appealing.

Psychologically I suppose I had now walked 'home', and so it was especially hard to gather the motivation to continue, particularly in such wet weather.

"What would be the worst that could happen?" I asked myself.

My answer was simply that I would get wet, and that really did not seem so awful.

I had been wet before, and I had the means to withdraw to my mother's house if I were to become too dangerously wet and cold.

I'M NO SHAKESPEARE

So I waved goodbye to my son, and walked into Plymouth city centre, where young adults, their lives ahead of them, were cuddled together under sleeping bags and blankets in shop doorways.

I bought a replacement gas canister and some cheap gaiters, before grabbing a cinnamon swirl and catching the ferry from the Barbican to Mountbatten.

Determinedly, head down into the horizontal rain, I continued to walk.

A cooked breakfast in a small and steamed up cafe at Bovisand helped to keep my focus fully on forward motion, and I soon arrived at Wembury Bay.

On a board beside the entrance to the National Trust car park was posted the telephone number of a ferryman.

No further than a mile ahead of me I would need to rely on this ferryman to take me safely across the river Yealm.

I attempted to call him but, due to no mobile signal, I was unable to make a connection.

At the brow of the hill the heavens opened and drenched me as thoroughly as if I had been standing under a power shower.

My new gaiters, which had so effectively been preventing any long grass from wicking water into my shoes, were now totally overwhelmed.

I managed to find a few bars of 4g and, by tucking my telephone inside my rain hood and leaning forwards, I left a message on the ferryman's answer phone.

I'M NO SHAKESPEARE

"Hello, I really hope you are running the ferry today! I am a lone coast path walker on my way to you now, from Wembury. Thank you!"

Billy the ferryman called me straight back.

"I haven't had anyone all day. Are you SURE you want me to take you?"

"Oh yes please! I DEFINITELY need you to take me!"

"Ok, I suppose I'll have to get the boat out then. I'll meet you on the jetty in fifteen minutes. Where are you staying tonight?"

"I have no idea"

"You can stay with me if you like"

"YES!!"

"I was only joking"

Billy was very good natured considering I had pulled him out of his warm and dry local to carry me safely across the creek.

He invited me to join him in the pub, but I needed to continue walking in the opposite direction towards the coast, to find a safe wild camping spot and to attempt to get warm and dry.

I feared that stopping now in the comfort of a pub would likely mean the end of the road for me.

Like a magician pulling a rabbit from a hat, Billy pulled out a present of a large bottle of cider and helped me to stuff it into my pack.

"You might need this, it's eight point five per cent." he said.

I'M NO SHAKESPEARE

He pointed out two wild camping spots on my ordinance survey app, with a shaky finger that suggested he may have just polished off a bottle or two himself.

I thanked Billy profusely through steamed up spectacles and nose dripping rain drops, before disembarking by swinging both legs over the stern in a decidedly less than lady-like manner.

The rain clouds parted, the evening grew brighter, and although my socks remained squelchy, a weak evening sun began to dry some of the dampness from my sleeves and hips.

I pitched my tent in a tiny quarry, a few miles past Noss Mayo, protected on three sides, and with a stunning view of the sea, over which the sun was now slowly starting to set in the west far beyond the Lizard and Land's End.

A wooden bench, no more than fifty metres from the quarry, offered a comfortable spot from which to swig my cider, straight from the bottle, and to watch wistfully as another ferry, laden with delicious croissants and delightful individual mini bottles of vinaigrette, sailed out from Plymouth.

Edward, a master furniture maker, had parked that evening not too far away from my quarry.

He was a keen local naturalist, and was out for his usual evening walk along the cliff path, with his binoculars and his dog, Hetty.

Edward stopped to chat, informed me that there were parent and baby peregrine falcons also living in the quarry, and kindly offered to bring me back food, or anything else I may need.

As tempting as it was to ask, stripping off and giving this very kind but complete stranger my clothes to take home to be tumble dried did not seem an entirely appropriate request.

I'M NO SHAKESPEARE

So, thinking on my feet, and as there was no mobile signal, I asked him if he could please just send an email later from his home, to let John know that I was safe and in good spirits.

In actual fact, Billy's cider had lifted my spirits no end.

I retired, still slightly damp, to my bed, and hoped that my body heat would dry me by morning.

DAY 51

Trench

It did, but the wind, which had begun to funnel directly from the sea into the quarry, had strengthened significantly during the early hours.

Two of my tent pegs were pulled free of the loose-soiled slate, which had not proved to be grippy enough to withstand the increasing force of the wind.

My centre supporting hiking pole was constantly being pushed away from the reinforced nylon and was encroaching onto my pyramid's rip stop fabric.

For the first time, I became scared of the very real danger of either catastrophic damage or of completely losing my shelter

Without internet I was also unable to check the wind forecast, and so decided to pack up my wet tent just after dawn and to walk on towards my next river crossing.

There was no way I could dry my tent in the windy conditions that took all my strength to simply stand.

I'M NO SHAKESPEARE

I held on tightly to my tent with one hand, to stop it being torn from me, whilst I removed each remaining peg.

The river Erme does not have a resident ferryman, and can only safely be crossed by wading, twice a day, an hour either side of low tide.

Low tide was predicted to be at 1423, so with such an early start I had plenty of time to dry out and to wait for the start of my safe crossing window.

I feasted on a super expensive lunch of super delicious pizza at the very comfortable Old School House Cafe at Mothercombe.

After finally managing to connect to the Internet I checked the upcoming weather forecast and discovered that fifty kph winds were now forecast for the next two days.

Billy also called me, to check if I had survived the wild night.

After lunch I tried not to slip on the seaweed, as I made my way, as reluctantly as a sheep about to be dipped, across the beach that was now exposed by the low tide.

At the edge of the sea estuary of the river Erme I removed my boots by hopping around one-leggedly, unsuccessfully trying to keep my socks away from the wet sand.

I rolled up my trousers to above my knees and stood, shoes in my hands, carefully inspecting the beach where the river dissected it.

Like my husband staring into the abyss of a car engine, I had absolutely no clue what I was looking for.

I asked a man, walking his dog, if he had any local advice on where best to ford the river.

I'M NO SHAKESPEARE

His reply did not fill me with confidence.

"You see the darker coloured water that looks like it's not moving?" he said.

"Make sure to avoid that area. It's where the deep trench is."

At least the water was not cold and it did not rise higher than just above my knees.

Its cleansing power was welcome.

It had been three days since I had last had a shower, or embarrassingly even removed my socks.

The small stones of the river bed offered a firm surface, but I trod gingerly as some were sharper than others and a trip would have been a disaster.

I should have worn my Crocs but it was too late now.

I held my breath tightly, especially as I got closer to the trench, and to the dark water that was being funnelled silently towards its depths.

Finally, safely traversed, I let out a huge sigh of relief and waved cheerily across at Doom Trench man.

Feeling like a true survivor, I set to the laborious job of cleaning the wet sand from between my toes, before I continued onwards towards Bigbury.

All of this South Hams coast holds a mixture of memories for me, some good and some very bad.

I remember childhood caravan holidays at Challaborough, skipping back from an afternoon of jumping from rocks onto soft sand, freshly caught mackerel proudly held aloft in both hands.

I'M NO SHAKESPEARE

I remember one bitterly cold January evening, with two female friends and our children, when we camped out under the stars on Wonwell beach.

A beach campfire warmed us, and my young teenage son and I shared a homemade tent made of tarpaulin and driftwood sticks, held down by rocks.

I also remember countless jobs, ambulance call outs, to the beaches, the roads, and the homes of this entire region.

Some of the trauma of the worst of these jobs still haunts me.

My hope was to walk through the area, my old patch, calmly with no unpredictable radio alerts and with time to reflect and to join the dots of all my experiences.

I wanted to seek a deeper understanding of how these traumas had affected me and even shaped my character, and to put them behind me.

In fact, by the time I had passed Torbay I had recalled far more buried memories than I had anticipated.

The beauty of the coast I walked through still hid a personal pain that occasionally brought me to tears.

At Mount Folly Farm above Bigbury I borrowed a mallet from a caravanner and made sure my pegs were as secure as they could possibly be in preparation for the forecast winds.

I carefully combined a packet of instant mash with a packet of minestrone soup, located a secret electric socket behind a fridge in the dishwashing room, and took my first shower since before travelling to France.

DAY 52

Hold on Tight

The wind overnight had been gusting at over forty kmh with squally rain showers, and even worse weather was forecast for the following day.

My tent was as safe as possible, pitched in a sheltered spot behind a hedge, my kit remained dry, and the farm was providing good free showers.

There was also a beach cafe a short walk away.

My friend, Helen, offered to come to rescue me, and it took determination to refuse her kind offer, and to stay put in my very sad looking pyramid, it's wildly flapping sides now bowed down by rain.

My daughter, Carly, is a primary school teacher in Kingsbridge.

She made a detour home after work to join me for tea in the beach cafe and we shared a blustery walk across the sands.

"You've got this Mum!"

I'M NO SHAKESPEARE

She hugged me goodbye and in doing so gave me all the encouragement I needed to continue to hold tight to my dream.

Buoyed too by a long shower before bed, a hot chocolate, and a torchlight escape into a dogeared copy of a Cosmopolitan magazine that I had found in the dishwashing room, and which promised to improve all manner of exciting things that I didn't really feel needed improving, I snuggled into my bag, with my hood pulled around my ears, and slept well.

DAY 53

Rescue?

The weak light of another day dawned.

A second day of enforced hunkering down in my tent, in a now empty field and with winds of over fifty kph blowing from all directions.

If I had not been tucked behind a hedge, protected from the full force of the wind, my tent would have been unlikely to have survived.

Despite my frustrations and stiffening legs I was glad I had decided to remain in place instead of continuing, just for the sake of covering a few more kilometres.

There would have been little to gain in continuing to walk, only to arrive with wet clothes and kit and to perhaps not have been able to find such a well sheltered pitch.

Being on a site was a great advantage over wild camping, especially in such weather, because there would always be the potentially lifesaving plan B of decamping to a shower block.

I'M NO SHAKESPEARE

It was also, once again, a lifesaver to have a groundsheet that could be pulled back to allow me to safely light my gas stove, out of the wind and rain, and to cook my porridge inside my tent.

A hot breakfast was always an instant mood lifter.

"It's VILE out there. Are you SURE you don't want rescuing?!"

Helen messaged me for the second time.

I held firm on the rescue, but very much looked forward to seeing Helen.

She promised to at least join me for a beach walk, and we shared a drink and some laughter later that afternoon in the Pilchard Inn on Burgh Island.

DAY 54

Gertrude

Finally, a calmer morning awaited me.

The dark clouds had cleared and the wind had abated.

After three days in one location my tent had created a tiny area of flattened grass, already beginning to yellow.

It felt good, comforting even, to pull on the familiar weight of my backpack, and I set off to walk carefully down the path from the farm towards the river Avon.

Wet grass and mud underfoot kept me extra vigilant, and I was lost in my own thoughts and concentration when Chris, the ferryman, strode past me.

Chris instructed me to wait beside the reeds on a small sandy spur of the river bank.

From there he would row out to fetch the ferry, and then would return to collect his passengers.

As if at a watering hole people began to appear and gather from behind bushes and reeds.

I'M NO SHAKESPEARE

Eight of us, all adults, a mixture of walkers, locals and holiday makers, climbed aboard the ferry and were safely delivered by Chris to the opposite bank.

Gertrude, the Swiss walker who I had previously met between Polruan and Polperro, was one of my boat mates.

She immediately galloped off at a rate of knots leaving me floundering in her wake.

I put even more distance between us by stopping at a Gastrobus on the Bantham estate, and ordering an organic and very delicious bacon and egg brioche and a huge mug of tea.

I remembered the tough surfer who I had once picked up from here, his ear partially severed from a collision with his board.

At Thurlestone beach I stopped at the beach restaurant and ordered a coffee, only to bump once again into Gertrude who was heading towards a bed and breakfast in Hope Cove, to be followed by two nights in a glamping tent in Kingsbridge.

Gertrude had allocated three months to complete the path in comfort, before taking her pre-booked flight back to Switzerland on the twelfth of October.

We walked on together to Hope Cove, and swapped WhatsApp numbers before parting.

Gertrude adores having her photograph taken and had ordered me to send her all the photos that she had been posing for.

My plan for the rest of the day was to reach Salcombe in time to take the ferry across the estuary to East Portlemouth, where I hoped to find a suitable place to wild camp.

Salcombe, as ever, was buzzing with visitors.

I'M NO SHAKESPEARE

A large percentage of its residences are now second homes and expensive holiday lets.

From Salcombe's history as a fishing village, its beauty and high street of designer shops now attracted affluent tourists, including lots of messing about on the water sailing types.

I had been hoping to catch up with the landlord of the Victoria pub, who had been a well-respected ambulance First Responder, with whom I had been involved in many emergency incidents in the town.

But time moves on, and the three young barmaids told me that pub had now changed hands.

I had time though to stop for a beer and a packet of crisps, and the women interrogated me about where I was going with my large backpack.

It was funny to see their awe and terror at the idea of wild camping alone.

"I couldn't do that. I would be far too afraid" one of them said.

The others all nodded in agreement, and I remembered myself at their age.

Would I also have been afraid?

I doubted it very much.

The dark, bad weather, insects and other animals, with the exception of snakes, do not scare me.

If anything, with age and life and work experience, I now know more about the seedy underbelly of society than I ever did as a young adult, but out on the path that knowledge does not scare me either.

I'M NO SHAKESPEARE

I can only imagine that a mirror might be the scariest thing on the coast path, if I were able, which thankfully I am not, to see my own morning reflection.

Once across the estuary, I climbed out of the woods, and the path opened to reveal the head of the beautiful Salcombe estuary.

This was a very quiet area after the last evening ferry to Salcombe had moored for the day.

A perfect clearing presented itself, and I knew it would be be unwise to hold out for anywhere more suitable.

My tent, pitched under a low tree, with the evening sun giving a golden glow to every leaf and a shimmer to the bay behind, was more beautiful than any human pose could ever be.

Not a soul passed by my idyllic camping spot, and my evening was one of total peace and harmony with nature.

DAY 55

Spear Gun

I left joyfully at 0830 before the first ferry from Salcombe had brought it's first passengers to walk past my beautiful camp.

All morning I passed just one dog walker, one jogger and one day hiker who were all walking towards me.

After a stop to read the interesting information, and to survey the sea through a powerful telescope at a coastguard visitor centre, I stopped at a bench a little way past Prawle Point, to prepare some chicken noodles.

It had been a long and remote walk, with none of the usual refreshment stops that I had come to rely on for energy and rest.

Tristan, my age, was a through hiker, walking in the opposite direction to me, from Poole to Minehead.

He was carrying a large pack and a large smile and as we approached we greeted each other in recognition of our similar status.

Tristan, despite the size of his pack, did not carry a stove.

I'M NO SHAKESPEARE

I was surprised as my stove is one of my most important bits of kit.

The comfort of a hot drink, soup or porridge at any time, and especially on waking, is worth the extra weight of carrying my stove.

Tristan showed me his wide mouthed water bottle in which floated a cold soaking coffee bag.

It is always interesting to talk to other walkers about their systems for storage, shelter, sleep, food, water, technology, clothing, and personal washing.

Tristan and I had both been eating wild blackberries, although now at the end of the season many were becoming too squishy, and full of unwanted extra protein.

"One cheek full of peanuts and one cheek full of blackberries" was Tristan's recipe for the best way to enjoy them.

I have not yet tried this genius concoction, and perhaps never will, but it did sound marginally more exciting than a sad plastic bottle of cold coffee water.

At Start Point I looked down into a cove where a seal was playing.

A man holding a spear gun stood beside me, with his Dachshund.

Bruce, my daughter's age, had been beachcombing and had just discovered the spear gun washed up and tangled in seaweed at a beach beyond the Point.

He described, frighteningly, how the gun had gone off and shot its spear just as he was freeing it, luckily without causing any deadly personal injury.

I'M NO SHAKESPEARE

Bruce was a very intelligent and interesting man to chat with.

He had his own boat and was a free diver for scallops.

He was also very patient and kindly answered my many questions about his work.

Bruce's intention was to attempt to reunite the gun with its owner.

We parted and soon met again by chance at Beesands where I was invited to join an outside table beside the beach, and to enjoy dinner with Bruce and his friend, a local veterinary surgeon.

My lovely daughter, after her work, drove once more to meet me, before depositing me at a very basic camping field, with no showers, no hot water, no electricity, no security, and which cost a very expensive fifteen pounds for the night.

I really should have wild camped

It was also a particularly cold night with the temperature dropping to just eight degrees.

DAY 56

Save Our Pub

Even the dew was colder than usual and my fingers grew numb as I repeatedly wrung out my thick dew wiping sponge.

It was then a short walk down the steep field back to the beach and then a steep climb up and over a hill to Torcross.

I stopped there for a cooked breakfast, and chatted with a holidaying couple at an adjacent table.

At the far end of Slapton Ley I stopped once again, tempted for a swim and a much overdue soapy wash in the calm sea.

My fantastic lavender and Geranium bar of all purpose hair and body soap, bought from the shop at North Morte farm still had plenty of life left in it, and even lathered perfectly in the salty sea water.

Feeling much cleaner, and with a new clarity of mind courtesy of my complete cold water immersion, I continued towards Dartmouth.

At every gate and stile on my way to Strete I was confronted with posters that stated, with an extreme urgency, "Save Our Pub!".

I'M NO SHAKESPEARE

Of course, I did what I could to assist in saving the town's pub by popping in for a lunchtime pint.

I enjoyed a great chat with Sue, a retired PE teacher from Plymouth who was enjoying a Saturday afternoon gin and tonic, and who had been tasked with the job of saving one of the pub's pot plants by taking it home to water.

From Dartmouth I caught a bus to Totnes, and then from Totnes a train to my mother's town of Ivybridge.

I spent three nights in Ivybridge, and travelled from there to attend the funeral of my dear client.

DAY 57

Stealing from a Charity

After three nights of sleeping comfortably on my mat on my mother's living room floor, my sister drove me to Totnes, from where I caught the first bus to Dartmouth.

The previous day, Gertrude had sent me a WhatsApp message to ask where I was on the path.

My break to attend the funeral had meant that our days now matched, so we met at a coffee kiosk before both catching the small car ferry across the river Dart to Kingswear.

We were about to tackle the section described as 'strenuous' between Kingswear and Brixham.

The morning passed quickly.

I was so engrossed listening to the drama of Gertrude's husband's affairs, and to the love story of her own ongoing affair with Grigio the Italian musician, that the steepest of ascents were barely noticeable.

At lunchtime we passed the bottom gate to Coleton Fishacre, a National Trust property and gardens.

I'M NO SHAKESPEARE

Focusing solely on the thought of National Trust cake we barely noticed the gardens as we climbed towards the cafe.

We stopped only once, for Gertrude to flirt with a BBC cameraman, his large fluffy microphone laid out on the lawn beside him.

What happened next was a surprising drama while standing in the tea room queue.

We had deposited our backpacks at one of the many empty outside tables, and were politely minding our own business, when we were approached and asked quite sharply if we were coast path walkers.

We smiled and nodded, and then it all started to go horribly wrong.

"You cannot sit here unless you sign in at reception. It is fourteen pounds each to be on the premises"

I tried to explain that we did not want to pay to enter the house, and that we really only wanted a cream tea, and would then be getting straight back on the path.

"You cannot sit in this cafe if you do not pay. It is not fair on the people who pay" was her chilly answer.

We were quite obviously perplexed, and reiterated that we only wanted a cream tea, that we were prepared to pay for, and that there had been no sign at the gate to stop our entry.

Gertrude was starting to swish her mane of red hair, and a de-escalation was called for.

I'M NO SHAKESPEARE

A compromise was found, whereby we paid a supplement for a takeaway drinking cup, and took our overpriced scones into the car park where a steep bank led to a very damp and mossy old bench.

Gertrude was indignant, and repeated that this would never have happened in Switzerland.

Things went from bad to worse.

We both re-entered the premises in order to return our trays, and to use the toilet facilities.

On our exit from the toilet, and about to head back quietly to the gate through which we had entered the gardens, we found our way blocked by the po-faced woman.

"You cannot walk back through our gardens. You will have to walk through the car park to another path".

Gertrude immediately saw red and barged past.

"I am going THIS way!" she asserted.

"You are STEALING from a charity!" shouted the employee, who by this time was beginning to steam at the nose.

I'm no statue of Aphrodite, but I stood, rooted to the spot, still trying to logically process this odd situation.

I had entered many National Trust cafes during my walk, and had never before been accused of criminal activity.

I love National Trust cafes, and had also never before baulked, despite it being a total daylight robbery, at paying seven pounds and twenty pence for one scone and a cup of tea.

Yet here I stood, confronted with an irate woman, whose day I suspected I may well have quite inadvertently completely ruined.

I'M NO SHAKESPEARE

I asked her gently for more detailed alternative directions to the coast path, whereupon she stated that if I wanted to return to my original gate I must first make a donation to the National Trust.

I replied assertively that in my view over seven pounds for a takeaway tea and one scone was enough of a donation, and repeated that there had been no such sign on the unlocked gate.

I eventually found my way back to the path, and continued over several more very steep headlands towards Brixham.

Still wondering what on earth had just taken place, I was nevertheless happy to once more be alone.

It would be almost another month before I saw Gertrude again.

At Brixham I camped at a caravan park, where I had been told via telephone that coast path walkers were given a 'special' price of fifteen pounds.

What I had not been told was that coast path walkers were also given a 'special' verge of grass on which to pitch, behind a parking area for campervans.

The verge, quite obviously by the odour of the cut grass, was also used as a dog toilet for the campervan owners' dogs.

The warm comfort and bonhomie of Brixham's rugby club, and its real ale, was only a short walk away.

I remained at the club until late, where I learnt of yet another huge storm that was due to hit the UK the following day.

My plans for the following day had been to wild camp somewhere past Babbacombe, but with the latest dire weather forecast I had decided to treat myself by booking the cheapest brick

I'M NO SHAKESPEARE

and mortar hotel possible, the totally thrilling Trecarn Hotel in Babbacombe.

DAY 58

Cabaret

Storm Agnes had been nicknamed "Angry Agnes" by the press.

She was supposed to have unleashed the most southerly tip of her ire on Torbay, but by the end of the day it seemed we may have been spared, as she raced on her way up the Irish sea.

I was relieved to leave dog poo verge, and retraced my steps quickly out to the path.

I descended into Brixham harbour via Berry Head, passing the sea pool where I remembered having swam as a child.

After a cooked breakfast at the harbour, I caught a bus to Torquay Marina.

I had walked this built up urban section many times and, for the sake of purity, I had no desire to methodically walk every tarmac and concrete step again.

From Torquay Marina to Babbacombe the storm clouds gathered, the sea state grew rougher, and I met very few other walkers.

I'M NO SHAKESPEARE

It was a good feeling, as I raced the storm towards Babbacombe, to no longer be living on the edge.

To know, that however wet I might get, there would be a hotel room to dry out in.

And what a hotel it was!

The huge Trecarn hotel was far, far past its heyday.

It has been used as a homeless hostel during Covid, and it now appeared to be a budget destination for coach holidays.

There was a huge reception area, with a bar and a dance floor, and every night was Bingo and cabaret night.

My room was basic, but perfect, and even had a full sized bathtub, which I took very little time in turning into a disgustingly filthy farm trough.

My wet tent and groundsheet were hung over wardrobe doors to dry out, and I surfaced from a deep late afternoon nap to the sound of music and chatter from the bar on the floor below me.

If you can't beat them, join them.

So, still wearing my tatty walking clothes, I descended into the ball room.

I was met by a buzz of glamorously dressed pensioners, sequins and Zimmers, and precious little space at the bar.

Despite its truly abysmal TripAdvisor reviews, and my concerns about how long it would be before there was a medical emergency, the Trecarn hotel was where it was at.

The cabaret man made a Bingo announcement.

"Five minutes til eyes down!"

I'M NO SHAKESPEARE

The excitement peaked.

Then a pin dropping, breath holding silence as the numbers were read out.

Followed by a collective groan when someone shouted Bingo on number eighty.

The stakes were high.

There was another holiday to be won.

I took advantage of the activity and attempted to stand up, wanting to reach the bar without being jostled by glitter topped people.

My legs promptly seized, and I narrowly avoided being the cause of the first medical emergency.

Everyone would have let me die though, because this Bingo was serious stuff.

The saxophone playing cabaret man sang his heart out, and I stayed at my table until the very end of the evening.

I was in awe of the energy and enthusiasm of the pensioners on the dance floor.

If this was old age then it really did not look too awful.

And was it wrong to slightly fancy the cabaret man?

DAY 59

Freedom

It was not until after I had boiled water on my gas stove in the bathroom that I remembered what the kettle in my room was for.

I returned my key and left a glowing review with the smiley, and slightly stunned, receptionist, who, judging again by the truly abysmal TripAdvisor reviews, was deeply un-used to such sincere five star feedback.

At Maidencombe beach I stopped at a wonderful cafe, ordered my usual cooked breakfast, and watched the wild swimmers, who were playing like seals in the post storm swell.

A ferry took me from Shaldon to Teignmouth, from where I checked with one of several coastguard officers that it was safe to walk the length of the sea wall beside the main line railway.

At a friendly cafe at the far end of the sea wall I learned the reason for the increased coastguard activity.

Two ambulance officers were in the process of waving off an ambulance crew, a patient with a head injury safely onboard and being cared for.

I'M NO SHAKESPEARE

They were both old colleagues of mine, and we were all surprised to meet again so unexpectedly.

One had already retired but had returned to the service after pension age to work part time.

The other was still a few years from his pension.

As I stood before them, tanned and tousled, no longer in uniform, no longer working twelve hour day and night shifts, and no longer their subordinate, I felt a huge and happy sense of freedom.

The summer campsites close to Dawlish were no longer open, so I had booked myself an Airbnb in the centre of the town.

To fill my time as I waited for the check in time to arrive I entered a local tea room where I ordered a pot of hot tea, and devoured two warm cherry scones dripping with cream.

Lele was a true German Hausfrau who kept a spotlessly clean home, and who wrote extensive lists of written rules for her guests.

The bathroom rules included only ever flushing the toilet with the lid down, and after each use of the shower it was imperative to juggle two different coloured microfiber cloths, a squeegee and a mop.

The rules held me securely, like a straight jacket, and I slept like a swaddled baby, not daring to hang my tent over the wardrobe.

DAY 60

Roseships

Before leaving to walk to Helen and her partner's home on Exmouth seafront, I sat with Lele at her kitchen table to drink tea and chat.

Being in such a well ordered but cosy kitchen actually made me a slightly homesick for my own home, to become a little less of a vagrant minimalist and to start nesting.

Lele had already been to the beach for an early sea swim and was tucking into a large bowl of muesli.

I was nervous however, of inadvertently breaching Lele's kitchen rules, and so I waited and bought a coffee and a Chelsea bun for my breakfast from a cafe in Dawlish.

"Oh, you look interesting!"

A man with spiky purple hair and facial piercings shouted across to me as we passed on opposite pavements.

From Dawlish to Dawlish Warren I followed another high sea wall and looked down onto the first dog walkers and beachcombers of the day.

I'M NO SHAKESPEARE

Trains passed close to me, a noisy blur of people of all ages travelling for probably as many reasons as there are grains of sand.

I watched them as if from another planet.

I had travelled to Minehead in that other world, by train and bus, holding on tightly to my brand new backpack.

My backpack had now become a part of me, moulded to my body, and my legs and boots had carried me over five hundred miles.

I wondered what those train passengers, if they had looked up and seen me, must have thought, if anything, of me.

Simon overtook me on the sea wall.

We chatted for a while and I learned that Simon had been a pool maintenance man and travelled widely with his work throughout the UK.

He had always preferred wild camping to staying in hotels and so had kept his tent, sleeping bag, and stove in his works van.

He recounted a time when he had inadvertently set up camp beside a river frequented by salmon poachers, and that a salmon had jumped and landed inside his open tent.

Simon's daughter lived in British Columbia in Canada, and he proudly told me how she had inherited his love of wild camping and was fully avalanche and bear trained.

From Dawlish Warren I walked along pavements and cycle paths to Starcross.

The Autumn leaves were continuing to fall, revealing rosehips and many other colourful berries.

I'M NO SHAKESPEARE

I found a YouTube video to check the safest way to eat rosehips, which are packed with vitamin C.

It is important to remove the seeds and the sharp filaments inside the hip.

This does not leave much that is edible, but I greedily licked off every bit of the divine tasting pink paste from my fingers.

From Starcross I caught the busy ferry across the river Exe, and sat beside Ian, a cyclist who was cycling a loop to and from Exeter.

We watched a seal basking on the sand banks of Exmouth harbour.

I reached Helen by lunchtime and was warmly greeted.

She had some unexpected time off work and, as she had done in North Cornwall, was planning to join me with her dog, Django, for another three nights of camping and four of walking.

After sharing cups of tea, and putting my clothes through the washing machine, we walked with Django from her apartment into Exmouth's shopping centre.

I bought a pair of Gel inserts for my boots, and an extra drybag.

My tent and ground sheet were also washed and re-waterproofed, which thankfully also removed the lingering scent of dog poo.

DAY 61

Quality Holidays

I had slept on the sofa after a long evening walk along the beach and a non-stop, catch-up chat with Helen.

At 0730, feeling as if I were on a stage, the floor to ceiling curtains opened automatically, revealing a sunny day and an uninterrupted panoramic view of the sea.

We retraced our evening steps along Exmouth beach, and stopped for a coffee at a kiosk, before climbing up toward the geodesic monument that marks the start of the crumbly Jurassic Coast.

We passed a huge holiday park where signs promised "Quality" family holidays in your very own static caravan, for a minimum price of thirty four thousand pounds.

I reflected on the huge old second hand Cabanon canvas frame tent that we had used for years when the children were small.

Cheap camping holidays with bikes, body boards, wetsuits, and tinned food, piled into a trailer.

I'M NO SHAKESPEARE

A seaside shanty home, where 'Quality' memories were most definitely made.

On our way along the coast I found a discarded grey hat, and promptly pocketed it.

My buff was good, but the colder evenings and early mornings would be more bearable with a beanie.

At Budleigh Salterton we stopped at a beach cafe, where we lunched like royalty on prawn sandwiches and actual salad.

Helen had been hoping for a night of wild camping, but we decided to stop at another huge holiday park at Ladram Bay.

Django donned his doggy pyjamas, and flopped immediately into his bed, not to move even an ear until the next morning.

I do also enjoy the unique peace of wild camping but, with the lighter summer evenings well behind us, anywhere with a warm bar was preferable to spending over twelve hours inside my bag in the dark.

We bought fish and chips from an onsite chippy, and I dragged Helen to Ladram Bay's huge clubhouse, which was heaving with excited families.

Our stay had coincided with the 2023 season's grand final of the children's talent show, and an eighties cabaret extravaganza.

Helen was traumatized.

I loved it all, and after a 'Quality' evening of cheering, clapping, and even some dancing around our bar table, we finally retired to our tiny tents.

Helen pretended to remain traumatized, but I think she had secretly enjoyed it too.

I'M NO SHAKESPEARE

How lovely it was, after three nights away, to crawl back into my not quite so fresh smelling sleeping bag, inside my delightfully laundered and re-proofed tent.

DAY 62

Hero Dog

We chatted with Rachel, a friendly home schooling mum, whilst enjoying our breakfast of freshly baked croissants, bought from the superbly stocked onsite supermarket.

Rachel was camping with her two young children, in the pitch beside ours.

The children were hopping about with excitement, about to paint pottery and to go swimming.

It was a steep climb up and over a mist covered headland before we arrived in Sidmouth just in time for a cooked breakfast.

We met Jim, a university security officer, who had just one year to go before his retirement.

Jim was already planning his own long distance walk, from Land's End to John O'Groats, to commence the day after he retires.

He asked lots of intelligent questions, and we wished him every success for his exciting retirement plans

"Are you walking for charity, or just for fun?"

I'M NO SHAKESPEARE

This question was once more fired at me from another couple who were also out walking in the cliff tops, as if the two things were mutually exclusive.

"If you would like to donate to charity, any charity, your choice, please do!"

This has become my stock response to the question that irritated me even more than:

"Have you read The Salt Path? Is that why you are walking?"

We stopped to brew coffee and we shared a protein bar at Weston Mouth beach.

Weston Mouth beach is now up there in joint first place of my favourite beaches.

I could have stayed there forever, reclining on its fine pebbles, far away from civilization.

My other favourite beach was another pebbly one, Peppercombe beach, my Qigong beach from where Weird Dutchman had fled in terror.

A young couple, evidently in love, were wild camping behind us, above the shoreline.

We watched as they emerged from their tent and ran giggling, hand in hand, towards the waves.

Even when in the sea, they were barely able to keep themselves apart.

We sighed with nostalgia, and pulled ourselves away from the idyllic beach, then set to climbing up and over another steep stepped headland.

I'M NO SHAKESPEARE

It had been a particularly strenuous day, and our plan to reach Seaton had been far too ambitious.

Our extended meal and beach breaks, however, had been worth every lost second of walking.

We googled a farm camping site near Branscombe and pitched there in a massive empty field, before walking another two miles along the lanes to the Mason's Arms, the local village pub.

It was Sunday.

It had also been a Sunday in North Cornwall, in the pub at Trebarwith Strand where we had enjoyed our first trail roast dinner together.

So, not wanting to break with tradition we ordered our second truly incredible roast dinner, vegan chestnut this time, and soon afterwards called a taxi to return us to our tents.

It was dark and the entire farm and camping field were now blanketed in thick wet fog.

Blindly trying to locate our tents by telephone torchlight was like attempting to find a needle in a haystack.

Django, however, was not about to let a little fog keep him from his pyjamas.

Nose to the grass, our little hero dog with his tail wagging euphorically at finally taking charge, led us safely home to our beds.

DAY 63

Poacher

After such a wonderful meal I slept as if on a virtual cloud, and woke to find that I was still pitched inside a damp and not so fluffy real life version.

No sooner had I sponged away the moisture, than my tent was once again drenched.

It was cold and disorienting, and I was glad of my new beanie which was pulled tightly down over my ears.

Carrying the extra weight of our sopping tents, we navigated carefully in wet boots through the mist to the cliff edge, then followed a woodland walk down and out of the cloud to the beach at Branscombe Mouth.

On our way there we met two perfectly coiffured and made up American women.

They had left their husbands behind in their hotel and were walking to Sidmouth carrying day packs, huge smiles, and an adventurous joie de vivre.

I'M NO SHAKESPEARE

We also met an older couple, who were walking wearing only light woollen clothes, no hats or waterproof layers, and carrying fabric daypacks and natural wooden walking sticks.

We stopped to chat with them and learned that they were also heading for Sidmouth, and were experienced long distance walkers.

After parting, Helen and I both had the same eerie feeling of having just stepped through a time portal.

In both their clothing and their speech, the couple had seemed to have come from another century.

The Sea Shanty cafe at the beach was certainly not a place to walk past without stopping for a cooked breakfast.

Helen also had an important business call scheduled.

We followed an undercliff walk to Beer, and continued across the pebbles and beside the colourful beach huts of Seaton.

All but one of the huts were closed and padlocked, but an older couple were sitting at a folding table in front of their open and beautifully organised and decorated beach hut.

We stopped to admire their style and learned that they actually lived in Lyme Regis, but that they far preferred the atmosphere of the seafront at Seaton.

"Lyme may be the jewel of the Jurassic coast, but the people here are far nicer" they told us

They had waited for five years before getting their hut, and spent as much time as they could there among their neighbourly community of other beach hut owners.

I'M NO SHAKESPEARE

During the winter months all the huts must be emptied, dismantled and carefully stored away from the damaging effects of the winter storms and flying pebbles.

In the spring the huts could be repainted by their owners, but only in pastel colours.

Seaton may not have boasted the grand architecture of Sidmouth, but the hut owner's enthusiasm was advert enough for the town's hidden charms.

We walked on along the main road from Seaton to Axmouth, and finally arrived at a caravan and camping park.

Disappointingly the only payment accepted was cash, of which we had none.

We shrugged and chose the only sensible option of heading to the pub next door, and using our debit cards to buy beer.

Burt, my age, was a poacher with a peaked cap from South Wales, who happened to be in the pub with his wife, Madge.

Madge had overheard us asking the barman unsuccessfully for cash back.

Without hesitating she had grabbed away Burt's freshly pulled first pint of the evening, and volunteered him to drive us to the nearest cash point machine back in Seaton.

Helen remained in the pub with Django and Madge, and I jumped up gratefully into the cab of Burt's decidedly fishy smelling white transit.

My great grandparents had been Welsh, so Burt and I were practically kin.

He was very amusing, full of dangerous stories and useful tips.

I'M NO SHAKESPEARE

Back at the pub, with our pockets full of cash, Helen got in the next round as a thank you, before we left to pitch up and to high five our luck at meeting such kind strangers.

One of Burt's tips had been for us to dine at the second pub in the village:

"Everything on the menu is good"

"But you can't go wrong with the belly pork."

So, belly pork it was, with extra crackling for Django.

The relaxed evening was unexpectedly fun and memorable, with great company.

For a night cap, we all returned to the first pub that was ideally located directly beside the entrance to our campsite.

DAY 64

Jungle

Three pints of local ale may have been a pint too much for both of us.

Waking up was tough, and packing our respective kit away was done in silence, with just an occasional painful groan from each tent.

Strong sweet coffee, and chocolate, restored our pioneer spirit, and we set off towards the start of the infamous 'Undercliff' section of the coast path.

The Undercliffs are a seven mile area of wooded wilderness situated on one of the most active coastal landslide systems in Western Europe.

The area has been described as the closest thing to a rainforest in the UK with its own warm and humid microclimate.

The walk is challenging, can be muddy and slippery, and follows a steeply undulating, uneven, and winding path through a maze of rock cavities, landslide and woodland.

Just the thing to attempt with a hangover, and fuelled by a totally inappropriate breakfast.

I'M NO SHAKESPEARE

At the entrance to the Undercliffs there is a warning sign that it is a severe and arduous walk that takes approximately three and half to four hours to complete, and that there is no access either to the sea or inland at any point.

We ploughed on gleefully, curious to enter this strange new world.

The description of "it can be muddy" was an understatement.

We squelched our way along mile after mile of wet claggy mud, only stopping once, in a jungle clearing, to refuel on mashed potato and minestrone and several more mini Twix bars.

Helen and Django were due to be collected from Lyme Regis, which was just as well for Django who by now resembled a swamp thing and would not have been allowed to sleep anywhere near either of us.

In a pub in Lyme Regis, fully recovered and ready again for beer and crisps, we slumped exhaustedly and waited for Helen's partner, Alistair, to collect her and Django from our second unforgettable adventure together.

Alistair delivered me to another very basic site in Lyme Regis from where I hugged goodbye to my dear friend, and air-kissed her equally dear but disgustingly filthy hound.

DAY 65

Hermione

I peered out of my tent at another morning of heavy dew.

The amount of water wrung out of my sponge was enough to fill a large water bottle.

For the second time during my journey my fingers became numb from the morning cold, and I was glad I had kept carrying the extra weight of my emergency gloves.

By the time I reached Charmouth beach I had fully warmed up, and stopped on a bench outside a beach cafe to drink coffee and to observe the early activity of dog walkers and joggers.

Now that it was October, the summer dog restrictions had lifted, and dogs were running crazily across the beach, sniffing new bottoms with gay abandon.

They were also chasing balls and digging holes, like children dizzy with the delight of being set free from class on the first day of the summer holidays.

To be once more alone in the silence of just my own thoughts was a stark contrast to the previous four days of chatter.

I'M NO SHAKESPEARE

Today I would be heading for Eype and West Bay, an area very dear to my husband who had spent many happy caravan holidays there as a child.

I was keen to send him photographs and to listen to him reminisce.

John's father had died before we married, and his mother was now in the clutches of advanced dementia.

As I looked back down at Charmouth from the top of the first headland, on my way to Golden Cap, I met a lady, my age, who was walking a red setter dog.

She told me that she and her husband had kept a static caravan in Charmouth for fourteen years, and for the lifespan of two dogs.

The site, however, insists on a new van after fourteen years, so they were going to have to give up their pitch.

Apparently the old vans get removed and "recycled".

It seemed to be that 'Quality' holidays could only be had in new vans, and that there was probably a 'Quality' profit to be made by breaking up perfectly good vans with quite possibly at least another fourteen years of use left in them.

Golden Cap is the highest point on the south coast of the UK, and the views along the coast in both directions, and also back inland are breathtaking.

I had been asked the same question many times by many people about what was the 'best' section of my walk, and it was a question I had never before been able to answer.

Everything is so subjective, and impressions depend greatly on the weather as well as on many other unique variables.

I'M NO SHAKESPEARE

I have seen beauty around every headland, and every beach and town has had its own special charm.

Even dusty, gritty Par with its backdrop of clay tips, and its proud and welcoming locals, whom I had met in the pub where I had camped, had captured a place in my heart.

This section, however, from Charmouth to Fleet, taking in Golden Cap, the sheer beauty and scale of Chesil beach, the uninterrupted views towards Portland, and the perfect balance of gnarly old benches, fields and ancient copses, was always and forever more going to be my answer to that question.

Descending from Golden Cap I reached the Anchor, which was a pub beside the beach in Seatown, a welcome watering hole for a pint of Golden ale and a Ploughman's.

Neil, my age, was a solution architect who stopped to chat as I carried on towards Eype.

"You are a woman of steel!" he repeated, twice.

He kept looking intensely into my eyes, and I suspected he may have been trying to flirt, until I remembered that the frames of my spectacles were now held comfortably in place by scrunched up pieces of wet toilet paper.

Neil did however ask for my full name, ostensibly so that he could read my book.

From Eype towards West Bay I sent many photographs to John, chatting with him in real time as he recalled more charming childhood memories of himself as a small boy.

Funny times preparing and cooking freshly caught mackerel on the beach with his father.

I'M NO SHAKESPEARE

Skipping with his parents and brother over the cliff tops to the penny arcades of West Bay, with coins burning holes in the pockets of his short trousers.

I had made no firm plans for where to camp that night, and was in the process of futilely asking an Amazon delivery driver for directions to the nearest campsite, when I was interrupted by Hermione.

Hermione was wearing a mini skirt and carrying a wicker basket.

"Are you lost?" she barked, with impressively clipped vowels.

I explained my desire to locate the nearest legal patch of grass on which to pitch my shelter, and we chatted.

"Come on. Follow me. You can camp on my lawn!"

Hermione was a force to be reckoned with, who, thirty years ago while in her early thirties, had trekked alone, carrying her own kit, to Everest Base Camp.

She had lived in her home in her beloved West Bay for most of her life, hanging onto it through thick and thin, and detesting with a passion the loss of community that resulted from second homes and the proliferation of Airbnb's.

Hermione's kindness knew no bounds, and I was wrapped warmly in her welcoming world of homemade treacle tart and tea, cider, and chats in her kitchen until midnight.

DAY 66

Chesil Beach

I had been instructed to pack up camp early, before Julian, Hermione's gardener, had a chance to identify the hobo who had been creating the bitch stains on her lawn.

Hermione insisted on setting me up for the day by preparing a good breakfast.

I sat at her kitchen table which was decorated with fresh flowers and a gingham tablecloth, while she plied me with organic oats with cream and golden syrup, and toast and homemade marmalade.

After breakfast we walked together back to the path, before Hermione turned towards to the beach for her usual sea swim.

We parted with huge thanks, took a selfie, and promised to keep in touch.

I stopped for coffee and cake at the very friendly and welcoming National Trust cafe at Burton Bradstock, where there were thankfully no guards with rottweilers to chase away backpackers.

The sheer size and wild beauty of Chesil beach took my breath away.

I'M NO SHAKESPEARE

The coast path includes a long and tiring section of shingle walking, where the cod fishermen heading for night fishing put me to shame.

The cheerful fishermen carried awkward loads that must have been three times heavier than mine.

They were trying to avoid the area where a trawler was working, with its long nets strung close to the beach it was blocking their chances for successful shore fishing.

At West Bexwith the entire beach car park had been commandeered by a film crew, and it was full of trailers and teeming with activity.

I stopped on the beach close to the car park, keen to observe the strange world of a film set.

I prepared a lunch of leek and potato soup, oatcakes, and pulled out a sweaty slab of cheese that I had saved from my previous day's Ploughmans.

I passed several more interesting beach and inland film sets as I walked, and for several hours a helicopter filmed as an old plane performed acrobatics above my head.

I met Roland, my age, as I was leaving the beach shingle.

Roland was walking a seven day section of the path and was heading for Abbotsbury, where he and his friend Bill were booked into a farmhouse bed and breakfast.

"Are you Cheryl?" he asked me before we had even introduced ourselves.

My reputation obviously went before me.

I'M NO SHAKESPEARE

It transpired that Roland and Bill had also bumped into Hermione in West Bay as she was returning from her morning sea swim.

She had told them all about Cheryl, somewhere on the path ahead of them, who had been camping in her garden.

Bill had apparently been floundering on the traverse of the hard shingle of Chesil beach, and had diverted to take a longer inland route to Abbotsbury.

Roland and I walked together.

At his suggestion, the plan was to ask at the farmhouse whether there was perhaps a spot of grass for me to camp on.

And then for us to all go to the pub together.

As we both approached the farm door I winked at Roland.

"Right, here's the plan. I'll be Wilhelmina and share your room. I'll leave my tent outside for Bill. You don't mind, do you?"

Roland opened his mouth to speak, but no words came out.

My request for grass had been refused, so I walked to the village pub and unsuccessfully attempted to charm a room, if I did not touch the bed, for half price.

It was not proving to be the most hospitable of villages, so I walked back to the path via the local Spar.

Whilst at the till and paying for my hot chocolate and beer, the lovely shopkeeper, who totally redeemed Abbotsbury, gave me some simple verbal directions to an unofficial camping hollow.

Without a map I got hopelessly lost, but met a couple walking four dogs who suggested I go on ahead and camp in their garden.

I'M NO SHAKESPEARE

It was a challenge to pitch between the piles of dog poo, but I was safe, and completely shattered after my previous late night of chatting with Hermione.

DAY 67

Bubble Bath

I walked past the Abbotsbury swannery a little after dawn whilst listening to the hauntingly beautiful classical music of a Spotify playlist entitled Lark Ascending Collection.

As a neared the village of Langton Herring I met Tamsin who was walking her dog, Musto.

We talked about how no one ever comes back from a dog walk, no matter how bad the weather, and regrets having gone out.

The countryside here was so quintessentially English with its sheep and cattle fields, deeply ploughed crop fields, pheasants, and ancient woodland.

Time appeared to have stood still, with nature and landscapes barely changed from the time of Constable and Turner.

Tamsin had recommended stopping for coffee a little further on at the romantically named Moonfleet Manor.

Moonfleet Manor is a refurbished Georgian manor house that is now a luxury family hotel.

I'M NO SHAKESPEARE

It has a large sign facing the path announcing a warm welcome to "All Coast Path Walkers and Pirates".

After paying a luxury price for my coffee, and spending an age at the sink in the luxury bathroom where I was playing with luxury hand wash and hand cream, I bumped into Roland and Bill.

Bill was sporting rogueish designer stubble and could perhaps have passed, at a squint, for a pirate.

We chatted and I headed off, leaving them both to enjoy the cream teas that they had inexplicably ordered without the cream.

Who does that?!

I would happily have licked off the cream and left them the scones.

I continued to Ferrybridge and onwards to Sandersfoot Garden Cafe where I ordered a pot of tea and my very own deliciously fully creamed and jammed cream tea.

My step daughter, Amy, and her husband, Mark, live in Weymouth not far from the path.

I walked to their house, where they had been expecting me.

Amy, who is a primary school teacher, checked her video doorbell twice, and then asked me for her grandma's maiden name and her father's favourite football team, before accepting that the vagrant at the door was actually me.

Mark, who is an Army sergeant and more used to covert undergrowth operations, simply ran me a hot bath full of bubbles and handed me a glass and bottle of white wine.

I love them both, and it was wonderful to be with my family again.

DAY 68

Portland

The Isle of Portland is an important part of the Jurassic coast, attached by the spit of one end of the immense Chesil Beach, and linked now to Ferrybridge by a road bridge over the Fleet lagoon.

Quarrying for Portland stone, prized for its use in the construction of many grand London buildings, was a major industry which, on a smaller scale, still continues.

I had borrowed a small day pack from Mark, and set off to skip, as light as a feather, around the coast path loop of the island.

Portland harbour was created in the second half of the nineteenth century, and is one of the largest man made harbours in the world.

In 2012 it was used for the Olympic Games.

I wandered through the impressive marina and Olympic sailing village.

It was a perfectly still and sunny morning, and recreational kayakers were busy preparing their equipment for a day on the water.

I'M NO SHAKESPEARE

From the marina I climbed an old railway track bed to Fancy's Farm caravan and camping site, where Sue served me a no-nonsense instant coffee for just one pound.

Her coffee was quite honestly better than all the fancy flat whites for which I had been paying a small fortune, including the previous day's insanely priced five pounds and six pence at Moonfleet Manor.

There has been a prison on Portland for almost two hundred years.

It was built to house adult male prisoners who were set to labour on the quarrying and construction of Portland harbour.

I walked around the barbed wire topped, high stone walls and tried to imagine the physical and mental torture of being confined to a cell.

From between the bars of their incarceration, could any of the prisoners on the high floors of that imposing edifice see beyond the high perimeter wall, towards the sea.

Did they dream of the day they too could walk free?

The Jailhouse Rock Cafe was a quirky place with a life size cut out model of Elvis standing beside the till.

I stopped there for a cooked breakfast before carrying on around the coast of the island, where the scarring evidence of old quarrying activities could not be ignored.

At Church Ope Cove I encountered my first collection of charming traditional Portland sheds, fell totally in love with them, and unhesitatingly decided to buy one.

I'M NO SHAKESPEARE

My romantic dreams were brutally shattered on discovering one of the six by four cabins for sale on Rightmove, with an asking price of 45,000 pounds.

Suzanne had been walking around the isle in the opposite direction to me, and was resting on a wall a mile or so away from the Portland Bill lighthouse.

She shared with me her addiction to long distance walking, and recommended taking six weeks to walk the Camino Frances.

I carried on towards a cream tea lunch at the cafe at Portland Bill, idly wondering whether I could survive on lager instead of ale, and what the Spanish equivalent might be to blackberries, pasties, cream teas, and cooked breakfasts.

Heading back towards Ferrybridge, stomach lurchingly close to the edge of the high sheer cliffs on the opposite side of Portland, I was rewarded with wonderful views westwards, over Chesil beach and the Fleet lagoon.

The land mass of the southwest peninsula of the UK disappeared into the early evening sea haze, and as much as I knew it to be fact, I found it hard to believe I had already walked so far.

A diversion through a stone sculpture park led me to the bus stop, conveniently placed opposite the oldest pub in Portland, from where I caught a bus back to Weymouth.

DAY 69

Rest Day

It was a Sunday, and it was seven days since I had last enjoyed a roast dinner.

Actually, apart from perhaps a fried mushroom, it was seven days since I had been anywhere near any kind of vegetable.

It was also eleven long days since I had last rested.

My boots were therefore discarded by the front door, and my toes were allowed to spread, sockless and free.

In twenty four hours the step counter on my telephone barely reached double figures, and I savoured every "Lionel Messi" second that I spent relaxing on the sofa, catching up with family and friends.

Amy was pregnant and occasionally nauseous, so Mark, who loved cooking, was preparing a huge roast lamb dinner for us all.

From the sofa I was also taking time to consider my next steps.

In four days, if all went to plan, I would be standing at the monument to mark the end of the South West Coast Path.

What then?

I'M NO SHAKESPEARE

I felt some creeping anxiety about re-entering the world that I had had so much fun opting out of.

Train and plane tickets needed to be booked, before I risked my marriage by simply turning and walking back to Minehead.

DAY 70

Smugglers

I had closed the front door gently, leaving behind me the evocative early morning aromas of toast and toothpaste.

Amy and Mark were both about to start the routine of another working week, but I was free, and walking calmly beside the glass-like sea.

With not a single ripple, its stillness was reflected in my thoughts.

Swallows were gathering, preparing to leave, and I wondered whether the prisoners on Portland saw them too.

Jean, my mother's age, was alone on the beach, serenely collecting litter in a bread bag attached to an embroidery hoop.

She told me she worked alone, quietly cleaning, both here and in the grassy areas and hedges around her home, a mile away.

At Weymouth harbour squawking seagulls, fighting over discarded fish and chip wrappers, broke the calm spell, and on the wide pavement of the sea front, I was stopped by Ken and Dick.

I'M NO SHAKESPEARE

The two men were about to return to Surrey from a "boozy boy's weekend" in Weymouth, and asked if I had walked far.

We chatted, and I learned that my dear Grandad's old village local, the Cock, in Headley, was also theirs.

At Bowleaze, set back a few metres from the path, I stopped in a cafe to enjoy the panoramic view down across Weymouth Bay towards Portland.

As I bit into a delicious fried mushroom, I spotted, racing towards Lulworth, the outline and familiar red hair of a Swiss walker.

Frank was a walk leader with the Ramblers.

He was very encouraging, and shared with me a second genius blackberry recipe, that had been told to him by another through-walker.

I will share it too, but with a caveat that, like a Chinese whisper, some of the original details may have been altered.

Ingredients: Freshly picked wild blackberries and a packet of cheap Custard Cream biscuits.

Step one: Use handle of walking pole to crush blackberries in multipurpose beaker.

Step two: Use multi-function penknife to scrape cream from biscuits.

Step three: Use Spork to gently combine cream and crushed blackberries.

Step four: Use fingers to delicately crumble biscuits and add as a topping.

I'M NO SHAKESPEARE

Shortly after midday I received a text message from Amy.

She had just returned from the hospital, where her twenty week pregnancy scan had revealed that her first child would be a boy.

Our second grandson.

At Osmington Bay I passed the perimeter of a large PGL children's holiday camp.

Years ago, as a part of his home education, we would often pack James off to PGL camps, including to this one.

He would usually sob dramatically on collection, wanting to stay there forever with his new friends and his adventure activities.

According to its website the Smugglers Inn at Osmington Mills was once the headquarters for seventeenth century smugglers.

They must have been very short smugglers, because I almost knocked myself out walking into a beam as I approached the bar.

A pint of Tanglefoot in the safety of the beer garden revived me, and I recalled having once sat there with John.

We had also shared a drink on the terrace after depositing James at the adventure camp.

Then we had driven to a bed and breakfast, for some child-free adventures of our own.

I continued on a rollercoaster walk towards a caravan and camping park at Durdle Door.

The sea remained calm and from the picture perfectly smoothed dips between the headlands I watched a tall wooden sailing ship heading silently towards Weymouth.

I'M NO SHAKESPEARE

It reminded me of the poem by Rudyard Kipling that I had just read on the Smugglers Inn website

DAY 71

A Canoe of my Own

I had camped in the 'Rookery' which was an area reserved for tents that, as its name might suggest, consisted of areas of level grass in-between tall pines.

The rooks made no compromise at all for campers, in fact they waged all out war by machine gunning tents from a great height, and squawking their displeasure for all but a few hours before first light

I now added tiredness to my disappointment that, due to its closure, I would be unable to walk through the section of coast path beyond Lulworth that comprises the MOD ranges.

I needed to be kind to myself, to rebrand my disappointment, and my threatening sense of anticlimax to not be walking the ranges.

My friend Rachel, who is a police sergeant, and who really should know better, helpfully suggested that I try crawling with my saucepan on my head and, wherever necessary, waving white knickers on a stick.

I'M NO SHAKESPEARE

I replied, firstly that my tiny camping stove, assuming I could even find a way to attach it to my head, would make me look like a performing monkey.

And secondly, that it had been far longer than I liked to remember since my knickers had ever been white.

Like saving a precious jewel in a box, to return to at a later time, I walked down to Lulworth Cove from Durdle Door, from where a taxi took me to Kimmeridge.

From Kimmeridge, on the far side of the closed section of the path, I looked back at the dramatic steep cliffs of the ranges.

They are only open to the public at weekends, and neither I nor my nerves could afford to have waited for another five days in the Rookery.

The weather had been dry for several days, and I walked on, over the crazy paving cracks of drying clay soil.

At St Aldhelms point I passed a plaque dedicated to the memory of Colour Sergeant George Meacham MBE.

The tribute resonated loudly:

"LOVE MANY, TRUST FEW,

ALWAYS PADDLE YOUR OWN CANOE"

From Winspit I diverted inland to Worth Matravers, where more whispers on the wind had informed me of the Compass and Anchor, a pub not to be missed.

Before reaching the village I caught up with George, who was a local resident and a retired metropolitan police officer.

I'M NO SHAKESPEARE

He provided good and humorous company as we walked together to the pub, and he pulled out his wallet to pay for my pasty and pint.

In the pub that had been in the same family for generations, and where there was no wifi or mobile signal strangers chatted easily.

George kept me entertained.

He was a great conversation partner, listening carefully as well as telling his own stories.

I had been lulled into a false sense of security, and was unprepared for his next unsolicited question.

"I bet out there on the path, you must have lots of opportunities for 'liaisons'."

I'm no Virgin Mary, but really?

I answered him immediately, without so much as missing a heartbeat.

"Oh gosh no, I'm far too dirty for that, but I have noticed that dogs seem to like sniffing my bottom".

I had obviously, and totally unintentionally, hit on a particularly fine fetish of George's, and his eyes lit up.

My canoe, like a trusty horse, was waiting for me outside the pub.

I paddled it far away from danger, to a beautiful and secluded last wild camp a few steps away from the sea ledge at Seaccombe.

There, safe and cosy inside my Pyramid, poignantly and for the last time, I fell asleep to the sound of the sea kissing the shore.

DAY 72

Headspace

I carried my porridge and coffee down to the rocky sea ledge, trying to imprint the memory of my last morning camping.

Overnight my telephone had somehow switched to French time, and I saw 0830 for the second time when it switched back to UK time.

Deciding that to be the perfect justification for two breakfasts, I ate my last emergency mini Twix.

My third breakfast was a fine full English at Durlston Castle, a mile or two before reaching Swanage.

For that final evening on the path I had booked a bed in Swanage Youth Hostel, but I would not be able to check in until 1700.

I googled the location of the town library which was ideally situated in the centre, and close to the hostel, and to several pubs.

I stood and stared, confused, at the sign at the entrance to the library room that read:

I'M NO SHAKESPEARE

- Kids
- Teenage/headspace

A librarian smiled at me benevolently, and asked if I needed any assistance.

"As I am no longer neither kid nor teenager, does that make me a headspace?"

She looked at me for a second too long, nodded imperceptibly, and pointed behind me and upwards to the stairs, where a hidden sign read "Adults".

For five hours I sat, gloriously ignored, upstairs in the adults' section, while my headspace was invaded by thoughts of the tsunami of civilization that I knew was racing towards me.

DAY 73

Trust the Path

As dawn broke, the sounds of footsteps and muffled voices increased, and the fire doors in the hostel corridor doors began to bang.

I switched on my private bedside light, and checked my phone.

More heavy rain was forecast, but not until late afternoon.

Nevertheless, I was impatient to start the seven miles of my final day.

Not wanting to wait for the town cafes to open their doors, I had paid for a Continental breakfast in the hostel.

I chose a sensible amount of vanilla yogurt, a rather less than sensible amount of mini pain au chocolates, and a banana, which I pocketed for later.

The atmosphere in the hostel was one of charged calm.

People and families of all ages were up early, and about to start all manner of adventures.

I'M NO SHAKESPEARE

The hostel was a beautiful old mansion house, with a wood panelled lounge and grand high-ceilinged rooms.

It was spotlessly clean, with genuinely kind and smiling staff who seemed proud and happy to be working there.

Swanage's golden-sanded, crescent shaped beach and safe, shallow waters are very close to the centre, and I could imagine how appealing the town must be as a family bucket and spade resort.

From the seafront I watched as if mesmerized, as a man, balancing skillfully on his elevating hydrofoil board, sped back and forth across the bay.

"He's not even wearing a life jacket!" a dog walker bent down to exclaim, to his dog.

On a residential street corner I met Frances as she was placing some rubbish in a street bin.

Frances was a very elderly lady who smiled at me gently as I crossed the road towards her.

We started to chat, and Frances told me of her early life as the daughter of missionaries, living in New Guinea and in Australia.

We talked about how for both of us 'trusting the path' was indeed a spiritual journey.

"May I walk with you?" she asked

Frances walked slowly beside me to the point where the coast path rejoined the beach from the streets of her estate.

"I never talk to anyone anymore, and hardly go out. I was meant to meet you today".

I'M NO SHAKESPEARE

Before we parted Frances placed her hand on mine, closed her eyes, and prayed:

"Jesus I pray for you to protect dear Cheryl and to guide her. She is so ready for you."

Actually I was feeling infinitely more ready for a hot bath and a cuddle from my husband, but tears pricked as I felt the poignancy of Frances' genuine kindness and sincerity, on this the last day of my journey.

As I descended the grassy field towards the Old Harry rocks a flock of trainee Nordic walkers were marching towards me.

"She's doing it wrong!" I heard one whisper, as I double planted my way down the hill to meet them.

We smiled and chatted, and many kind and curious questions were asked by all members of the walking group.

It is almost always a pleasure to answer people's questions, and I always try hard never to rush, or to show them that their questions have been asked countless times before.

I stopped for a last coffee, and my hostel banana, in the Salt Pig Cafe.

Laying on the ground at my feet, as I stood to leave, was a perfect fallen acorn, still in its beautiful cup.

The acorn is the sign for the South West Coast Path that I had been following for the past three months.

I thanked it for keeping me safe, and hoped that it would grow into a mighty oak tree, to outlive us all.

As I started to walk the length of Studland beach I ticked down minutes instead of miles.

I'M NO SHAKESPEARE

It was as if my every sense, including the sound of the small waves lapping against the shore, and the feel of the fine sand against my roughened soles, was heightened

I helped a grandmother to search gently for shells.

She told me that her dear granddaughter lived near Luton, far from the sea.

Whenever the child visits, she asks to sit with her grandma, to create art with the shells that she knows her grandma will have collected, especially for her.

There is a section of Studland beach that is reserved for naturists, where large beach signs warn the clothed that naturists, like dolphins or golden eagles, "May be seen beyond this point".

There, in the dunes, I slowly removed and placed my clothes over my backpack, and I walked out and across the sand towards the water's edge.

The sea, as deliciously cold as silk, enveloped my body, and I swam.

I swam in carefree circles in the clothes that I had been born in.

I had tasted freedom, and I cried, and I laughed, at life, at death, and at this whole crazy, beautiful adventure.

Acknowledgements

Firstly, I would like to give thanks to my husband, John, for his patience and unfailing support.

I am certainly no Marie Condo, and I may not always be easy to live with, but I would not be me without you.

To my mother, Anne, who was simply always there for me, and who never once wrinkled her nose.

To my daughter, Carly, for her boundlessly bossy support, and for her complete belief in her old mum.

To my mighty agent and sister, Stephanie, I have no words other than heartfelt love and gratitude.

And finally, to the blackberries, who for three months provided my sole supply of dietary fibre and antioxidants, and to which I attribute my robust good health.

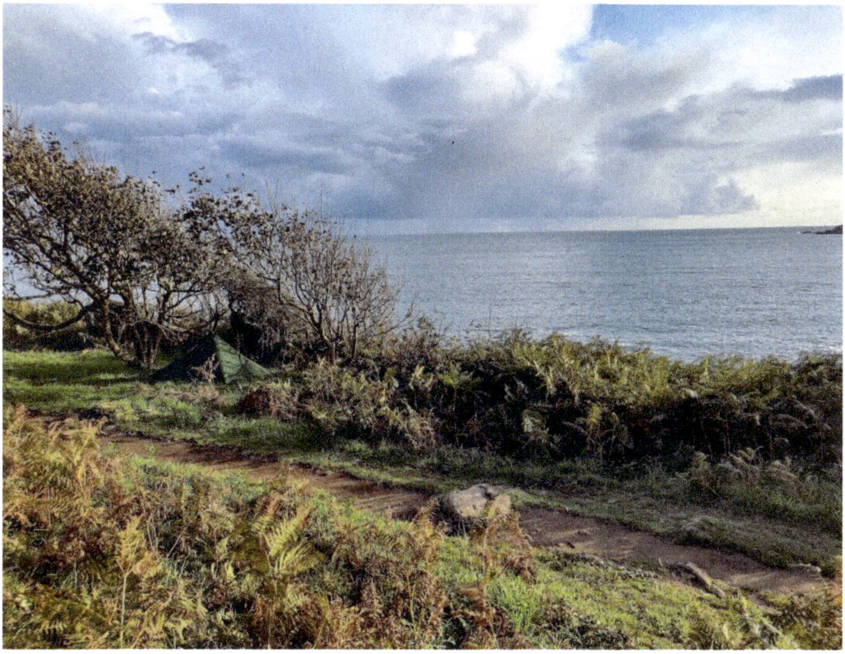

Printed in Great Britain
by Amazon